Children With Learning Differences Exploring Artmaking to Address Deficit-Laden Perspectives

A volume in
Promoting Justice, Diversity, and Inclusivity Through Arts-Based Practices
Christa Boske, *Series Editor*

Promoting Justice, Diversity, and Inclusivity Through Arts-Based Practices

Christa Boske, *Series Editor*

The Time is Now: Creating Community Through Social Justice Artmaking (2022)
    Christa Boske

Children With Learning Differences Exploring Artmaking to Address Deficit-Laden Perspectives

Christa Boske

Kent State University

INFORMATION AGE PUBLISHING, INC.
Charlotte, NC • www.infoagepub.com

Library of Congress Cataloging-in-Publication Data

A CIP record for this book is available from the Library of Congress
http://www.loc.gov

ISBN: 979-8-88730-398-7 (Paperback)
       979-8-88730-399-4 (Hardcover)
       979-8-88730-400-7 (E-Book)

Dedication

Art is possibility.
Art is hope.
Realize the depth of your strength.
And,
all you bring to the world.
You have the power to make meaningful change.
And guess what?
You did.
You had this within you the entire time.
You are the pebble.
Make the ripples.

—Christa Boske

Contents

Using Artmaking to Express Being Misunderstood, Undervalued, and Marginalized

Christa Boske

*D*o we show up for students with learning differences? If yes, how do we show up? If now, why not? How do we celebrate student excellence? The purpose of this book centers on empowering students who were often underserved in schools due to differences in how they learned. Together, they utilized artmaking and their first-tellings to express their insights, lived experiences, and hope for the future of schools.

Children With Learning Differences Exploring Artmaking to Address Deficit-Laden Perspectives, pages ix–xx
Copyright © 2024 by Information Age Publishing
www.infoagepub.com

Authors wanted to make this clear. They do not, will not, and prefer society does not use the term "disability" when referring to learning. Authors prefer the term "learning differences" or "learning challenges" be integrated throughout this book versus "learning disabilities." Why? These authors suggested the term "learning disability" focuses on an individual's "cognitive weaknesses" versus "strengths" and often isolates them from other learners. In the school they attend, authors stress how teachers and school leaders commit themselves to using the term "learning differences." Authors highlight they simply learn differently than many of their peers.

You are excellence.

You matter.

You show up.

How do we show up for you?

You know who you are.

Do we know you?

Do we think you cannot learn?

Do we think less of you?

How often I hear,

"Oh no, not these kids . . . they can't do that kind of work."

Do we believe in you?

Do we know your spirit lights up a room?

Do we know how you persevere?

Do we admire your determination?

Your inner strength?

You know you have something to offer.

Do educators believe this?

How do we show up?

How does this negative imagery show up in our self-talk?

How do these beliefs show up in your self-talk?

Am I enacting power to those I serve?

Are you bigger than this system that attempts to bring you down?

What you think.

What you feel.

This should matter to learning.
To my learning of self as an educator . . .
Mentor . . .
And champion to all of those I serve.
—Christa Boske

I wrote this poem after working with a myriad of school communities expressing frustration and concerns with children in need of special education services. What judgements do you think students, families, teachers, and school leaders with learning differences have experienced in school?

Like other marginalized groups, students with learning differences were often segregated and offered minimal to no education. Did you know children with learning differences could be placed in asylums where they remained hidden from the eyes of the world (see https://mn.gov/mnddc/parallels/one/1.html)? Unfortunately, it was common practice not to provide children with intellectual, social, and physical educational spaces for development. The education of deaf and blind children in the United States was an outcome of more inclusive views of human potential, and by the early 19th Century, this perspective resulted in the education of individuals' "disabilities" and/ or emotional disturbances. A common public sentiment at the time centered on the belief that students with learning/social-emotional differences may harm other students, demand more attention, cause disruptions, and cause a feeling of awkwardness in the classroom.

After World War II, disciplines such as sociology, psychology, and social work were coming into their own. Along with this growth came a surge in new research and programs directed toward students with "disabilities." Families also worked hard in both schools and the courts to ensure that their children had adequate educational opportunities. Their efforts paid off in 1975 with the passage of Public Law 94–142, the Education for All Handicapped Children Act.

That legislation established five key principles of special education (see https://www2.ed.gov/about/offices/list/ocr/docs/edlite-FAPE 504.html):

1. No child with a "disability" will go without a free public education that is appropriate for them; to disallow them this education is to violate their constitutional rights.
2. Nondiscriminatory education is based on the Fifth and Fourteenth Amendments of the U.S. Constitution. According to this principle, children shall be assessed fairly so that they can be placed in appropriate classes. This principle includes nondiscriminatory education for African American and other racial minority children.
3. Free and Appropriate Public Education (FAPE) states children shall have an education that is based on an accurate diagnosis of their needs and with programs designed to meet those needs.
4. Least-restrictive environment (LRE) ensures students with "disabilities" do not become unnecessarily segregated from their peers who attend general education classes. This suggests students should be educated with those who do not have disabilities to reduce the chances of their feeling isolated.
5. Procedural due process gives power to those who have disabilities so they can challenge decisions made by the school regarding their education. An impartial tribunal hears these challenges, with counsel and witnesses taking part in the process. School records are also available for reference. Families have the right to appeal decisions with which they disagree.

The Education for All Handicapped Children Act (see https://sites.ed.gov/idea/IDEA-History) gave states federal funding to educate students with "disabilities." But these children were segregated from their nondisabled peers and often lost access to much of the equipment and many of the programs found in general education classrooms. In 1991, this law was changed to the Individuals With Disabilities Education Act (IDEA). According to the federal Office of Special Education and Rehabilitation (OSER), the federal government, through IDEA, serves approximately 6.8 million children and youth with "disabilities." In order for youth to be served, these students must exhibit characteristics of one or more of the federally recognized "disabilities" in order to receive services using IDEA funds.

By knowing and upholding these laws, school communities may ensure they provide meaningful educational experiences to students with learning "disabilities." To deepen our understanding of challenges still facing families and students, I created two fictitious scenarios aligned with narratives of student authors, families, and people who serve diverse school communities in the United States:

School Psychologist: "We really can't help your child until we assess him in functioning in a classroom?"

Parent: "My child cannot manage sitting in a regular education classroom at this time. He has been bullied, put down, and isolated because of the challenges he faces. Right now, he attends a school to help him manage his learning difference and mental health. Pulling him out of this school and mandating him to sit in regular education classrooms for days on end for the purpose of you observing him is not in his best interest. If you can explain this to me, I am open to trying to understand your perspective."

School Psychologist: "That's mandatory and not up for discussion. This is the only way we do an assessment."

Parent: "I don't understand. Why would you put a child in a public school, in regular education classrooms for days with complete strangers when he is struggling to understand what is being taught...how it's being taught...and dealing with his anxiety and depression...and you want to watch him spiral?"

School Psychologist: "We can't just take the word from the psychologist and teachers from the school."

Parent: "That doesn't make sense. How is this mandate in the best interest of my child? Why would you set him up to spiral and emotionally fall apart in class?"

School Psychologist: "We don't look at it that way. If you want your son tested, this is what needs to happen. Hopefully, he won't fall apart. We don't expect much from these students."

Parent: "I want to make sure I understand this. You 'hope' my son doesn't fall apart? You are willing to put my child at risk? I will take this to the next level. My child has been harassed and bullied for his learning difference...anxiety and depression. You are not putting my child in regular education classrooms and leaving him there to fall apart. That is not acceptable. Who will fight for my child?"

This fictitious scenario is a compilation of conversations with a myriad of families and students requesting their children be assessed for special education services. As families grow more concerned for their child's social-emotional welfare, they may feel alone. They may see the standard of learning lowered because their child "cannot do" what "regular ed students" are allegedly capable of doing in classrooms. Families in search of supports for their child are available; however, families may not be aware of federal laws and resources available and designed for their child's situation. Failing to provide special education services for students in need, especially those who are vulnerable and underserved, prevents students from gaining access to programs and resources essential to attaining academic success (see Morgan & Farkas, 2018).

Here is another scenario to consider:

Children sit at their tables and read books. Sometimes people who are not familiar with children with learning differences may not understand how to meet the diverse learning needs of children served in schools. They may assume all children learn the same way—sitting at tables and quietly reading to themselves. Some students track words with their fingers while others read out loud or quietly to themselves. However, at one table, a child wears headphones and listens to the words from a book read by a narrator. Everyone is reading. They are reading at their appropriate level as well as being given resources aligned with the child's learning.

The student in this fictitious scenario was diagnosed with dyslexia, a learning difference characterized by difficulty reading. In order for this student to receive meaningful accommodations to support the development of her reading skills, the student received a legal designation for a learning difference, which is identified as an individual education plan (IEP). Without appropriate educational resources and a supportive environment, students may experience feelings of being lost, frustration, and confusion. Simply put, some students' brains work differently than her peers. Most importantly, understanding children's learning differences do not influence a child's intellect is also critical to their development.

Students who receive special education services enroll in special education programs due to mental, physical, social, emotional, and/ or behavioral differences. Federal legislation governs special education services across the United States through the Disabilities Education Act (see https://www.ada.gov/). This legislation guarantees students receive a *free appropriate education* and works to provide students with opportunities to learn alongside their peers in the *least restrictive environment*. The number of students with learning/behavioral/emotional differences has increased from 6.4 million in 2011 to 7.2 million in 2020–2021 (see https://nces.ed.gov/programs/digest/d21/ tables/dt21_204.30.asp). In the United States, approximately 14.5% of all students Ages 3–21 received special education services. However, these statistics may vary according to the state in which the student is served. For example, 11.3% of students are served in Hawaii while 20.5% of students in New York received special education services (see https://nces.ed.gov/programs/digest/d21/tables/dt21_204.70.asp).

In addition to the number of children served in special education, statistics regarding the racial identity of the students also tells a story: White students 14.9%; Black students 16.8%; Latinx students 14.1%; Asian students 7.6%; Pacific Islander students 11.6%; American Indian students 18.6%; and biracial/multiracial students 15% (see https:// nces.ed.gov/programs/digest/d21/tables/dt21_204.50.asp). Where students attend school seems to matter. Black and Latinx students who attend schools with a majority of White students are often overidentified for special education services. The overrepresentation of students of color in special education, with the exception of Asian students, suggests American Indian students are twice as likely to receive these services and Black students are 40% more likely (see https://www. ncld.org/wp-content/uploads/2020/10/2020-NCLD-Disproportionality_Trends-and-Actions-for-Impact_FINAL-1.pdf).

Students who have an IEP may be told by school officials they have a *disability*. For the purpose of this book, authors contend students are not *dis*-abled. In other words, they are capable of learning. Students just learn differently. Therefore, the term *difference* is intentionally utilized throughout this book. Authors requested this term (i.e., difference) be used throughout this book to be culturally responsive versus the term disability, which is often perceived as a negative term by these students. These *learning differences* encompass a myriad of students diagnosed with disorders, who are in need of specialized support in order to reach their academic goals. Student authors contend utilizing the term "difference" honors the way their brains work.

Did you know roughly 1 in 5 students in U.S. schools receive special education services? Authors in this book experienced a myriad of deficit-laden language, bullying, harassment, and were often undervalued in their schools. Why? Students received special education services due to their learning differences. When thinking about the rights of students, families have legal rights when their child is diagnosed with a learning/cognitive/social/emotional/physical difference. According to the Office of Civil Rights (2022), states have a responsibility to ensure a free appropriate education and schools are required to respond to bullying or harassment with an immediate and appropriate investigation to eliminate a hostile learning environment.

On the other side of the spectrum, some students may be disproportionately represented in special education: children living in poverty and children of color. Students who live in poverty are often over-identified in subjective categories like intellectual and emotional disabilities, and therefore, placed in separate classrooms. These special education services are often inferior to the quality education received by their regular education counterparts (see Morgan & Farkas, 2018). Once students are diagnosed with a "disability," children living in poverty and children of color often experience lower expectations and lower academic outcomes (see Schifter et al., 2019). Furthermore, children receiving special education services are frequently situated in classrooms with teachers who have less experience in language arts, math, and science. Although students are diagnosed with mild "disabilities," special education services are viewed as ineffective for many students (see Dever et al., 2016). For example, Brown and Black students experience inequalities at a higher rate than their White counterparts with negative outcomes often associated with receiving special education services: negative stereotypes, racial segregation, group misrepresentation, and deficit-laden thinking (see Skiba et al., 2016). Therefore, inappropriate special education placements in programs such as these may not lead to favorable student outcomes. As disparities continue to raise concerns regarding systemic racial bias due to schools possibly ignoring potential system-wide factors influencing higher rates of over identification, especially for children living in poverty and students of color (see Tatter, 2019).

Integrating the Arts

Artmaking may seem "more fun" or a "superficial" method of occupying students. However, artmaking is a powerful process of thinking through situations, reflecting on experiences, and learning is possible (Robinson, 2013). For these students, artmaking provided spaces to address the challenges they face as young people. Having a learning difference provided students with opportunities to express themselves through multiple mediums. They gained confidence along the way. Artmaking provided imaginative spaces, especially for young people who may feel challenged by traditional teaching methods. For these authors, art was a dynamic intellectual discipline encouraging them to think, problem solve, and construct their own ways of knowing.

Overview of Chapters

This book begins with Max's chapter "More Feelings... I'm Laughing" in which he expresses his understandings of Paulo Freire's work and its influence on him as a learner. His artmaking reflects how he utilizes the concept of a "puppeteer" to share his commitment to empowering with learning differences. In Chapter 2, Hannah writes about the significance of opening doors in "Feeling in the Middle." Hannah encourages readers to make meaningful connections with others, the significance of listening, and the need to understand each other, hopefully, growing from those new ways of knowing. In Chapter 3, which she titled "Alone," Chloe discusses how her artmaking empowered her to share aspects of herself that were often "lost in the shadows" and therefore, these feelings may "take a toll on you." She ends the chapter recognizing she has so much to offer the world and identifies herself in a new light. In "Injustice," Chapter 4, Amiah takes the reader on a journey about racism and the power she felt by engaging in this social justice-oriented artmaking. She stresses the significance of educating ourselves, accepting one another, and taking time to understand what Black people face every day in the United States. Hunter, in Chapter 5 titled "Learning 'Dis-ability,'" emphasizes the unexpected power he felt engaging in this social justice-oriented work. He shares the influence of the process on his sense of self as well as a significant increase in his confidence as a student with dyslexia. Madison, in Chapter 6 "Make or Break," stresses how often she feels judged by others for parts of her identity. In Chapter 7, "We Have a Lot to Lose," Alex encourages readers to pay close attention to what is on the minds of young people: the environment. He wants people to understand how often students think about the world, care for the environment, and feel compelled to make meaningful change. The book concludes with Chapter 8 reviewing significant messages from student authors who recognize the need for artmaking to promote voice, especially for those who have been marginalized because of their identity.

Conclusion

In this book, authors share their diverse experiences in special education. They understand these services are ideally designed to support their learning; however, these authors often experienced bullying, harassment, lower expectation, which influenced their sense of self, confidence, and aspiration for employment as higher education (see Bal et al., 2014; Cherng, 2017). Being placed in special education programs that are ineffective and often engage in deficit-laden practices, may lead to more severe and frequent disciplinary action (see Camera, 2017) and less time in the classroom (see Cooc, 2017).

Authors suggest these trends occur too often in schools. Their first-tellings suggest the need to improve the overall quality of the educational services children placed in special education and to utilize artmaking as a means of expression. To avoid bias, deficit-laden practices, segregation, harassment, or bullying, there is a need for policymakers to interrupt these practices, provide meaningful teacher/school leader preparation, engage in culturally responsive practices, and ensure those making decisions are culturally diverse (see Ford, 2012; Ford & Russo, 2016).

Student authors contend art and learning differences go hand in hand. They emphasize the need for artmaking for social justice to be integrated throughout the curriculum, and for students with learning differences, there are no exceptions. For these authors, artmaking was beneficial, empowering, and promoted freedom. They were able to think and respond differently. Authors also recognized their artmaking could take a myriad of forms. What was most important? The message played a significant role in their artmaking. They gained independence, increased confidence, and developed a stronger sense of self. In this space, they excelled. Artmaking was inclusive and empowering.

References

Bal, A., Sullivan, A., & Harper, J. (2014). A situated analysis of special education disproportionality for systemic transformation in an urban school district. *Remedial and Special Education, 35*(1), 3–14. https://doi.org/10.1177/0741932513507754

Camera, L. (2017, August 31). New study questions links between race, disability in students. *U.S. News & World Report.* https://www.usnews.com/news/education-news/articles/2017-08-31/new-study-questions-links-between-race-disability-in-students

Cherng, H. S. (2017). If they think I can: Teacher bias and youth of color expectations and achievement. *Social Science Research, 66,* 170–186. https://doi.org/10.1016/j.ssresearch.2017.04.001

Cooc, N. (2017). Examining racial disparities in teacher perceptions of student disabilities. *Teachers College Record, 119,* 1–32. https://eric.ed.gov/?id=EJ1123434

Dever, B. V., Raines, T. C., Dowdy, E., & Hostutler, C. (2016). Addressing disproportionately in special education using a universal screening approach. *Journal of Negro Education, 85*(1), 59–71.

Ford, D. Y. (2012). Culturally different students in special education: Looking backward to move forward. *Exceptional Children, 78*(4), 391–405. https://doi.org/10.1177/001440291207800401

Ford, D. Y., & Russo, C. J. (2016). Historical and legal overview of special education overrepresentation: Access and equity denied. *Multiple Voices for Ethnically Diverse Exceptional Learners, 16*(1), 50–57. https://eric.ed.gov/?id=EJ1108022

Morgan, P. L., & Farkas, G. (2018, May 4). Are too many minority students identified as disabled? Or are some who need services overlooked? *The Washington Post.* https://www.washingtonpost.com/news/answer-sheet/wp/2018/05/04/are-too-many-minority-students-identified-as-disabled-or-are-some-who-need-services-overlooked/

Office of Civil Rights. (2022). *Disability discrimination: Overview of the laws.* U.S. Department of Education. https://www2.ed.gov/about/offices/list/ocr/disabilityoverview.html

Robinson, A. H. (2013). Arts integration and the success of disadvantaged students: A research evaluation. *Arts Education Policy Review, 114*(1), 191–204. https://eric.ed.gov/?id=EJ1022287

Schifter, L. A., Grindal, T., Schwartz, G., & Hehir, T. (2019). *Students from low-income families and special education*. The Century Foundation. https://tcf.org/content/report/students-low-income-families-special-education/

Skiba, R., Artiles, A. J., Kozleski, E. B., Losen, D., & Harry, B. (2016). Risks and consequences of over-simplifying educational inequities: A response to Morgan et al. (2015). *Educational Researcher, 45*, 221–225.

Tatter, G. (2019, February 21). *Low-income students and a special education mismatch*. Harvard Graduate School of Education. https://www.gse.harvard.edu/ideas/usable-knowledge/19/02/low-income-students-and-special-education-mismatch

1

More Feelings ... I'm Laughing

Max Oeflein

I t was interesting. It was something new...something different...I guess it was something new and something I never talked about. At this school, teachers and students are the same. I have been at other schools. Another school was different. It was a public school and it was different. They were more like teachers were higher than students. It was like silence. I stayed quiet. I didn't tell them how I felt and they didn't ask. It wasn't every class, but it was some classes I was uncomfortable and some classes I was fine. I came here in 7th grade. I had quite a few friends, but some of the teachers were uncomfortable. I was silent.

Children With Learning Differences Exploring Artmaking, pages 1–7
Copyright © 2024 by Information Age Publishing
www.infoagepub.com
All rights of reproduction in any form reserved.

I wrote a poem and I don't do this, but I just did and it's not something I do outside of class, but here it is . . .

I talk here.
I keep my thoughts to myself.
I am a quiet person.
I keep my feelings to myself.
When I did this art,
I exposed my feelings.
It was interesting.
It was fun.
I don't remember the last time I had fun sharing my feelings.
It was out of the ordinary.
I would do it again,
But it would depend on the topic.
In the end,
I felt excited.
I was excited about the work.
People said it was cool,
My parents, of course.
I just smiled.
I just smiled big.
I am surprised.
It's pretty cool.
People thought I was in graduate school.
I have never been told that by anybody.,
That's new.
My art influenced people.
That's cool.
That's pretty cool.
Yeah, that's pretty cool.

I had a big smile when I read this poem I wrote. I guess I am happy. There is a poem about me and it's nice. It's really nice. I never had a poem about me. I think it's weird to have a poem, but I like it. I don't give myself compliments. I don't even remember the last time I said something nice about myself. I can't even remember. I don't know. It feels good. It's cool.

If I were to meet new teachers. I want them to know my art tells them to help their students, listen to their students, and know we are equal. Tell them what you are struggling with. Let students know. And go in early and get help from students and realize kids are experts too and know things they may not know about. That would be pretty cool . . . to have students to help them. Students are asked for their opinions here and how they can help and that's cool. That didn't happen in my other school. Maybe it happens in some classes, but I don't think it happens in many,

I went to the gallery. My mom and dad went with. They were super excited I had an art piece in the gallery. That was quite an achievement. When I walked into the gallery, I was nervous and excited. I never thought what it would be. It is always different than I think it would be. When I saw it, I was proud.

My art was called "The Puppeteer" (see Figure 1.1). My social justice issue was teachers think they know more than their students and have nothing to learn from them because they are just kids. My social justice stance was that teachers and students should be equal because they can both benefit from each other.

I never heard of this before. It's just not talked about, I guess. Maybe they don't want to talk about it because some teachers and principals want authority. They might want power over someone else. When I am respected and have power, I feel good. I didn't know what I wanted to do for my art, but when I heard of it, it was interesting and new. I didn't know about this.

Definitely, there were teachers who did not treat me like an equal. This was before seventh grade. When I messed up, they were kind of mean. I mean when I had to do a band, and perform the C scale, I had to go in front of the whole entire grade and I was so embarrassed and I obviously messed up. I couldn't do it and I didn't like the band and I didn't practice. I didn't practice because I didn't like it. I just got Fs and I got yelled at. That was pretty good for that class. At least I got a C. I didn't understand anything in any class anyway. School was hard for me. Band was the worst class for me. It humiliated me. He humiliated

Figure 1.1   The Puppeteer.

me. I hated it the most. The other teachers were nice, but I didn't learn anything. I was in the lowest classes and needed the most help. I was in those ones. I was told that I wasn't gifted and I was told I was the lowest. I don't know. I knew I was smart and I wanted to be in my friends' classes. I knew I was smarter. I felt left out, I guess. I was bummed, but I did have a band and lunch with them, but I didn't like the band.

When I came here, it was much better. I am in honors classes. I am in smaller classes. And I understand things better. I knew I was smart. Teachers here treat me like I exist. It feels good. It feels much better. I want to feel like I exist and not like I don't.

I learned about this guy named Paulo Freire. He believed that teachers and students should be equal. He wrote a book about it. If you had it in your hands, then you might go to jail. The government didn't want anyone knowing that teachers and students should be equal. If students knew things, they could start a riot or something or ask questions. And if they did that, the government would be in trouble and might be overruled. I agree with Paulo Freire. Teachers and students need to learn from each other and should be equal.

The hand would represent the teacher. The puppets need to be the students. The teachers are controlling the students. But what if the teachers are controlled by the principal? And what if the principal is controlled by the Board of Education? And who controls the Board? The government...so the strings control each hand under the other hands and on the bottom are the students. So, the big hand is on top and it represents the government. I will use real string from the hand on top. The Board is made of several people. The string goes to the Board members. The Board members go to the principal. The principal goes to the teacher. The teacher goes to the kids. The red background represents power. The equal sign represents how everyone should be equal. The tape over the kid's mouth represents how you can't talk and you have no opinion. The book Pedagogy of the Oppressed is about how students should be equal to teachers and how the teacher controls the students' thoughts and that students are treated as passive objects. The photo of the students raising your hands represents an old school way of thinking and how it seems rigid to me and not relaxed.

If I could go back and talk to teachers, I would tell them, well, that they should not have people performing in front of everybody. It's embarrassing. Maybe teachers need to do a better job explaining some of the topics. There were other kids like me at the school and they weren't treated very well. So, all kids should have been treated equally.

I came up with this art because of the different levels of authority in schools. The government controls everyone and that reminded me of being the big hand and making the big decisions. But I took it to another level because it just doesn't stop there. The Board of Education is controlled by the government and then the Board tells the principals what to do and the principals tell the teachers what they will teach…how they will teach…and what they will learn. So the people at the very bottom are the students. That's not right.

If I made my art about what is right, the strings would be cut. There would be no strings. All of us would be on the same level. We could all do one big circle. That's one way of seeing it. You could only know who is who if I labeled them. Otherwise, it doesn't matter because we are learning from each other. I don't know if there are any schools where teachers and students are equal. I just looked it up, but all I found was about money or race or teacher to student ratio, but nothing on Paulo Freire's work. And then, I found a Paulo Freire school in Philadelphia, Pennsylvania. It would be different to go there. We would be equal. It says there is love, critical thinking, diversity, and equality. Those are what they believe. That school is a big fan of him. There are four campuses with 2,000 students and 89% of the schools are Black and Latinx…100% of the students receive breakfast and lunch and that's pretty cool…and 86% of the graduates go on from their second year of college. These schools are focused on social justice. That's pretty cool. It's different. But these schools seem to be by just one person…at least that's what I found. I would want to see what it's like and to see what it's about. I couldn't go there, because it's too late, but I could learn about it.

This school that I go to is about learning differences and Freire's schools are about social justice. It's all about getting the word out and having voice…and having education for students in urban areas who don't have money…we have people focus on us going over our learning differences and that Freire school teaches them about equality and social justice. That's cool.

If I were the head of education, I would try to get more schools to be like Paulo Freire. I want them to be equal and stuff. I would hope schools would want to be more like this. I would have to change a lot of stuff...what they teach...it's really bad...especially history...that's really bad...especially on certain topics...that's really important...knowing history...it teaches you what happened in the past so we learn and it doesn't repeat itself...and there are important people who did and do really important things and we need to know about them. There are people who aren't in our books. They are not there. They exist, but someone made the decision to take them out, like Black History.

2

Feeling in the Middle

Hannah Cohen

his whole thing was very relaxing. I feel I got my message across when I made my art. And I am proud of myself. I feel relaxed looking at it. I like the way the colors meet. I saw an image that resembled two faces meeting in the middle. I took the concept of two faces meeting. I think it symbolizes understanding, empathy, and love. There is no gender associated with these faces. They can be whoever you want them to be. I wanted them to be unrecognizable, but as human. I don't want people to give them an identity they may not share. If you see someone on the street, you might think you cannot identify with them. But when you can't see someone's race, class, orientation,

Children With Learning Differences Exploring Artmaking to Address Deficit-Laden Perspectives, pages 9–15
Copyright © 2024 by Information Age Publishing
www.infoagepub.com

or gender, you can connect with someone. It's not about shutting doors, it's about opening doors. I also opened the door by not letting people be able to identify with an identity. I wanted the colors to represent feelings. The shapes are mixed all together.

You never truly feel one thing at a time. You don't just feel all things all the time. They are connected. I wanted saturated colors. Maybe blue is sadness. Red may feel like anger. Pink is embarrassing. Green is envy or disgust. Yellow is happiness or excitement. The dark purple is sadness or depression, like the darker places in life. The orange in the middle means they are sharing feelings with one another. I wanted that color to pop out because that's the focal point of the painting—the connectedness of two people. I also feel like this painting represents how I have grown in high school. I feel like I have grown about understanding and learning about people and being open. It's been difficult, but mostly happy and exciting. I had trouble letting myself be open at first. I was worried people would not take my feelings seriously. As long as I treat people with kindness, I realize they will in turn treat me that way as well. I learned to treat people with absolute kindness. These emotions are what I felt going through this journey and learning about myself and others.

Sometimes I have one or more ideas, and if I don't like it, then I combine them or I work around the idea and find things I like or don't like. But for this piece, I had an idea and moved forward on it. I had trouble gender-neutralizing the characters in the painting and images... and wanted a more platonic rather than romantic love. I don't believe all love is romantic and not all of them have to be physical.

My Artmaking

If I did this art again, I think I would have changed the shapes. I might think them through, but it would not have turned out so naturally. The messiness does compliment my ideas around feelings or emotions. These aren't puzzle pieces that fit in a nice package. These are shapes that are of their own and they don't fit. They're messy... and some are even jagged.

I don't paint. I do more drawing and sketching. I also use clay or collage. I have focused on social justice in my later high school years.

I learned some people need support and education on some matters. Social justice has not been something I did in my art until now. I feel a little more educated and in tune with myself. All students should have this opportunity. It was freeing and it gave me power. This power was something I didn't feel before now. I feel I can make better art work. In the past, I did art to make myself happy. Now, I realize I can make art to say something... to say something important to me... things that need to change.

And now, I would like to create more social justice art and more art for others.

This is my art abstract for the exhibition:

Social Justice Issue: People are dismissing people based on who they are and discriminating against them based on their opinions or problems that they face.

Social Justice Stance: People need to learn how to be empathic and listen and value what people are facing in their lives.

I truly value empathy, I think it's one of the most important things a person can give. Once I started high school I noticed a lot of my friends were angry, sad, or depressed. They didn't want to talk about their feelings at all and it felt like they were wearing a mask over who they truly were. I started asking what was wrong and started to listen to them more. I tried to understand how they felt and give them as much support as I could because I care about them more than anything.

I feel that most people don't want to get involved with their friends' feelings because it can be sad, infuriating, or an inconvenience to them in some way. Friends take love, support, and work, and I am willing to do all three.

I don't feel I have been listened to that much in my life. I have not been heard by the most important people in my life like family or my old teachers.

When I was at my old school I was used to people telling me, "You are not good enough," "not smart enough." It feels so strange that no one thought of how I was feeling after they would say such things. When I heard these hurtful things, I felt dumb, wrong, and like I had no hope for myself. The only way I knew how to express my feelings

Figure 2.1 Feeling in the middle.

was through anger or sadness. I didn't know how to control my feelings or how to express them in a positive way.

It wasn't until I started to see a therapist when I was 13 that I learned how to be kind to myself and listen to myself when others wouldn't. I feel like I have been thriving ever since and I want to make others feel the same. So I listen and care about others as much as I can.

No one told me it could be easier or less painful if I had someone to talk to. This probably means most people feel the way that I did and didn't know how to express themselves either, which is really sad to me.

I had a rock in my chest and I couldn't talk to anyone about it. But once I found the words and the right people, I feel like I can do anything and the people around me would support me. I am very proud of myself and of my friends because of who we have become as people, and I am so grateful to have them in my life.

My Advice for People Who Want to Listen

What do teachers need to know? My advice is to first be a friend to yourself, give yourself empathy. Because you don't want to go around helping others when you haven't helped yourself first. Listen first and ask questions to the people around you. Ask simple questions and listen much more than talk. You could make someone's day if you just ask how they're doing or tell them you appreciate them. Just do little things, they could mean the world to someone. Even if it inconveniences you, it's important to know that no matter what, it helps people way more.

The colors in this piece represent all different types of feelings and emotions people can have when sad, conflicted, angry, or happy. The two faces meeting in the center of the painting represent that they understand each other. They understand what the other is feeling and truly care about their feelings. Where they meet is the only space on the canvas that is orange to show how truly important it is to learn and help the people around us. Also all the colors on the canvas swirling and mixing together represents how difficult feelings can be and how they change over time.

I hope my art and my story inspires people to listen, learn, and understand as much as someone can. I don't feel people are ever done learning. There is always something new to learn or to understand. So get out there and start learning!

My Future as an Artist

I have not often done this type of work, I mean, social justice art. I should do this more as an artist. But sometimes, it is difficult to solidify my feelings or my thoughts on paper. I am afraid that what I do may not come across on the canvas or painting. I am afraid of what I feel. I heard from other artists that I should not be afraid of my feelings. I have been told to make art as much as I can even though it might be considered bad sometimes. I have made bad art once or twice. I know I'm not supposed to say that, but sometimes I feel that way. I should believe in myself more. But it's hard for me to keep them, the bad art, and learn from what I didn't like. But I can use that as a reference for the future.

After doing this art, in the future, I think I would do something on community justice. Everyone needs to come together as a community. So many people feel alone, but when you come together, as long as you try, the more people can achieve greater things. When you are a big group, you can accomplish more. But if you are alone, you don't feel you can do this, but there are people out there. I think an example would be like community violence like robberies or jumping and fist fights… protesting or educating or informing people in political power about situations. And when you have a community, a community of voices, then it's not seen as a problem, but as a solution.

Another issue might be hate. It doesn't have to be physical. You can hurt someone by saying mean things or spreading false information throughout the community. I think social justice art has helped me look at this work differently. I want to focus on love, not hate, education, and acceptance. This is what my future social justice art would focus on for me. Just because you don't understand something, doesn't mean you have to hate it.

I believe making this art and writing about it helped me get my feelings out on the canvas. I am the same person because I feel these things are important. I learned about myself. I can do this work. I have a voice. I am important even though sometimes I don't think that way. I learned something about myself. The difference is having the courage to take it out of myself and put it on display for other people. People saw me. They actually *saw me*. One person at the exhibition even asked me to get my picture with my art. It felt like being a real artist and being recognized for doing something meaningful… in a way that it affected other people.

I mean, I am a real artist.

That was the first time I felt that way. It felt nice.

I think other students should feel this way, especially students with differences. We don't often get a chance for people to believe in us, but we do matter. We matter a lot. I think other people should put their art out there and see how their art can influence other people.

Maybe my art can help you...or students...or schools. Just maybe. Just maybe my art will get you to think.

Conclusion

Art should be included in schools. It is a way to get your feelings out and to be open and to be relaxed. It's the only place I can think of where you can be absolutely creative. Art can be anywhere. It would be easier for students who are more creative to do something with their hands instead of taking a test and regurgitating whatever the teacher taught. I learn best through someone talking to me directly and hands-on. Being personal with teachers helps.

This social justice art helped me do that. I was personal. I let it all out. It felt good. It felt really good. I shared my story. I shared what it is like to be me...what is important to me. That I matter. And all students matter, but they don't always feel that way.

I was able to wear how I feel on my sleeve. It didn't feel scary. It was empowering. I had freedom. I was able to make my own choices and work at my own pace and be able to interact with my classmates. I don't usually get that outside of art. This project was more personal. It also felt comforting because my art was valued and loved. Talking to my classmates and my teachers really helped and inspired me for my future work. And this was hands-on because I could mix and move the paint and put it on the canvas the way I wanted. There was no right or wrong answer like there are in school sometimes. Some might say there is a right and wrong outside of art, but not here. Not with this project. Not with this social justice work. There wasn't a right or a wrong. Everything I did was acceptable and exceptional. It has to be from your heart and in the case of social justice, have a meaning and tell a story.

3

Alone

Chloe Schlenk

I don't think I have ever been presented with the opportunity that portrays for a lack of a better word, "fixed in the world." There are a lot of injustices to a lot of groups and a lot of ideals, but there really shouldn't be. There seems to be premeditated hate. And you grow up this way and it's hard to change that. A lot of the world grows up like this. And then you can't change that. It is my responsibility as part of this younger generation to help other people realize you can't do this or act this way. It's an opportunity to learn what like really is happening within these communities or these individuals. I think we need to step back and just kind of see how we can approach injustices from a different viewpoint or

Children With Learning Differences Exploring Artmaking to Address Deficit-Laden Perspectives, pages 17–24
Copyright © 2024 by Information Age Publishing
www.infoagepub.com
17

perspective. We need to step inside and be insiders. It could either mean that you are part of a community and it's part of your identity like being born that way like a deaf community or LGBTQ community or you can be a supporter of those communities. You may not be a member, but you can understand where they are coming from. This is what empathy is...I think it's sometimes you might be born with it or something you learn. Like you can learn to love others, learn to love others different from you, or you go and you be a part of this community especially when the world doesn't think their voices are important enough.

Honestly, I am not sure how empathic I am. I try. I honestly try. I don't want to be hateful. There are people who are homophobic or antisemitic, but I can't empathize with those points of view because my heart is not full of hate. I think it's about me putting myself out there a lot. I grew up with a generation very connected with the internet. And when you do that, you are anonymous and you put yourself out there and let people know what's going on. You can do that on the internet. I think the internet is complicated in the way it works. It can be used to hate and cycling it back, but there are places where you can learn and grow and meet new people. It gives you a moment to say there is a world outside of your own experiences. Just because you see the world in your limited way doesn't mean the rest of the world is like that. I just have to see myself in the shoes of others. It's hard to describe. I hear scenarios that could be an absolute nightmare if I experienced that. And knowing that, it makes me not want that for other people.

I think that just being in rough places myself makes a difference. I have a lot of privilege, but things don't always go right for me. I think about what doesn't happen for others. I just grew up with a childhood history of mental illness: depression, anxiety, and ADHD. The public schools gave me an environment that took a toll on me. It was just like a lot of things, I guess. I could never keep up with homework. I was exhausted. I would get yelled at. It was too much for me. There are a lot of noises and things going on in school. I was in sensory overload. I would get nauseous and sick all the time. I went to school every day feeling sick. I didn't know why I felt that way. Why was I always sick? I knew I had a mental illness, but I didn't know the specifics. In second grade, I couldn't pay attention at all. And a few months later, I was diagnosed with ADHD. For a long time, I have been on medication. My depression and anxiety are things I cope with over time. I put myself in the right environment and learned to do that so I can thrive. That environment is one that I can be myself. It sounds simple, but it's not. I can't be bombarded with lights or noise or bumping into lots of people. Basically, not a public school. In public, I think there is always somewhere I can go to take a breather. The hardest part is being subconscious about being with people. In public school, I am in the building and in class and I can't just leave. I can't just take care of myself. It's much more difficult to take care of me. I have more control when I am in public or outside of school.

I work hard. It's just like getting out of bed. Just going through the motions of getting out of bed and actually getting out the door is helpful. It gets me in motion. I can actually do what I need to do and not overthink it. If I allowed myself to lay in bed, that's what would happen. I coach myself. It's like being a military general to myself. I have to tell myself I will get up. I usually get dressed and eat just like everyone else. Nothing special, but I do have to be militant. Sometimes I am mentally stuck in the mud. I scroll through the feed on my phone instead of taking a shower or getting dressed or being in motion. It becomes a distraction, but most of the time the distraction doesn't win. If the distraction wins, I either need someone to pull me out of it or get a notification on my phone or my cat comes in and wants to pay attention, but it might need to be an external factor.

I think I am really lucky to be surrounded by people who want to support me and do support me. I realize there are people who don't have that in their lives. *How does this help you become more empathetic?*

When I started this artmaking, I wanted to imitate a feeling of isolation and helplessness. Being in a state that you want to reach out, but there is no one there to help you. I think it came from my life. I had a really really rough time in middle school. I was clinically depressed and for some reason I thought I had to do this on my own. It's not true, but that's what I thought. And I had to learn that I cannot do this on my own. I realize this is true for a lot of people. I think depression and anxiety isolates you to an extreme. It doesn't have to isolate you physically, but you can choose to do that. It isolates you mentally. You are just stuck in your own mind. I lose a connection with others. You are in such a dark place that you don't think anyone can help you or that no one would understand or nothing could be done or that anyone would care enough to be there. I learned that part of me needed to let

Figure 3.1 Alone.

people in and let them help me or support me and the other part of me needed to realize that I was responsible for getting myself up and out and in an environment that was good for me, a place I could be successful. I created this piece to bring to life the feeling of isolation and unfamiliarity.

I am in a different place now. I don't know what the future holds, but I can tell you that I am okay now. I think having more people support me and being in a better environment for myself really helped. I let people in now, and that took a lot for me. It was hard, but I am really fortunate to have people in my life who take time to support me and care about me. Some of those people are my friends and family. I got some medical help and seeing therapists helps and being on medication helps too.

Here's my art abstract, the one I put up for the art exhibition:

Social Justice Issue: Often, people who identify as LGBTQ (lesbian/ gay/bisexual/transgender/queer) are in need of protection because they hide who they are.

Social Justice Stance: LGBTQ people should be able to be who they are and feel safe to be themselves.

I have a lot of friends who are in the LGBTQ community. It is hard for them if someone finds out...what if someone from my family found out...how would this impact me? I care about minority groups because they are people just like me. I have been through really hard times and it doesn't feel right that they would have to be treated differently and go through something so hard.

I have had a lot of internal issues with mental health. I have had depression on and off since fourth grade and I have ADHD (attention deficit hyperactivity disorder). I didn't know it then, but looking back at it now, I realize I saw a lot of that in a younger version of myself. I started getting diagnosed with depression early on, but I don't think my family was looking at that early. We were really just looking at attention so we really just focused on that. I didn't really know what that meant. I just knew I wasn't happy and that I was struggling in school. I felt isolated from others. I felt like sometimes that I was the only one going through it, but I knew it wasn't true. I felt like I was on my own little island.

I am really lucky to have parents who kinda supported me through all of that. That's how I knew, but I didn't know any other kids so maybe that's why I thought I was on an island. My memory on it isn't too clear, but I did kinda distance myself from people too. Yeah, I still do that. I find myself getting myself in the cycle again. I do this because I see myself as a burden to them. Even now, I feel uncomfortable about this. I am used to keeping this stuff to myself. I was so lucky to have support from other people. I can't imagine what it is like not to have that support. If I told them I was stressed and they told me I was wrong, I can't imagine what that would be like. I feel like I have to kind of get that strength within myself to support others. This art can be the start of finding that within myself.

I am not used to all of these compliments. I am hearing that it's kind of silly, but I trick people into thinking this way about me, like if I'm nice, did I trick them? Am I really nice? I feel like from the person's perspective, they are authentic, but it's like the game of telephone sometimes. I don't hear it the way they intended it. The message gets warped almost. When I heard Christa tell me I was insightful and brave and courageous, it's like an automated filter in my brain. I know she meant it because she doesn't have anything to gain from saying it, and she doesn't want anything from me, so I know it's how she feels, but my filter is saying that deep down, unknowingly I am kind of manipulating people. Deep down, maybe I don't really mean the things I say. When I say these out loud, those people shouldn't feel bad and they tell me it's just my brain messing with me.

> *When I think about me,*
> *I don't know.*
> *I don't hate myself.*
> *I study zoology.*
> *Animals have always fascinated me.*
> *Humans can talk and you can figure them out,*
> *but animals are different.*
> *They don't realize they are in a community.*
> *They live in their own moments,*
> *in their own lives,*
> *but animals have simplicity.*
> *They have unconditional love.*
> *Some are tricksters.*
> *Some are arrogant.*
> *They don't pass judgment.*
> *They can fly.*
> *They can swim.*
> *They don't have anyone telling them they can't.*
> *But we have unwritten rules*
> *and sometimes we follow them,*
> *but they don't make sense.*
> *Animals don't have to wonder about the meaning of life.*
> *They think about how excited they are to see people*
> *Or*
> *When is the next meal?*
> *Or*
> *When do I get to go outside and see all the pretty birds?*

They aren't dumb.
They just think about the world a little differently.
We say things like
"You are not smart."
I am smart.
I am smart in my own way.
I am empathic.
I am a good listener.
If I really love something,
I put my all into it.

I see a lot of really passionate people who are LGBTQ community who just want to love themselves and be a part of a community. I see myself in those people. I hide aspects of myself too. When I hide that, there is a lot of scary things out there and when you keep that world inside of your head, it becomes like a looming shadow. It's like you are trying to find a source of light that you can take a moment and relax and breathe, but if you are lost in the shadows, then you are going to get lost and it's going to take a toll on you.

Conclusion

This is not an everyday conversation, bringing things like this up. It's nice to kinda do this. I want to make this art about others, but I am realizing this is about me and I am kinda getting this out there. I am not used to this. I realized what a relief it was to get this out . . . to use my art in this way for the first time, really. I create a certain facade and it is exhausting, absolutely exhausting. I don't think this is uncommon. It should be, but I think there are other people who feel this way too. If you had to act like you were British, and you knew everything about having green grass, well, it's hard because it's all about keeping up appearances, right, and what people think of you. I want people to know I am smart. I want people to know I matter. I think. I think a lot. I don't want anything to stand in my way. I won't be in the shadows. I am standing in the light. Well, maybe, I am the light.

I don't think there is an instant solution, but we need to start a conversation. That's what I am doing right now. My art is starting that conversation. I am using my story to relate to the LGBTQ community and we can use these ideas to relate and understand one another. So, my art and my story can help me talk about this right now because I know there are people out there who will understand me, but other people, such as people who are LGBTQ, may not have the privilege I have to do this art and to talk to people. Are you going to start a conversation using my art? Using my story? I hope you do.

4

Injustice

Amiah Robinson

I am bringing awareness to this world to let them know the world is unfair to people of color all around the world. The purpose of my chapter is to help you understand that social justice art is powerful and I used this to bring attention to this huge problem and that it's not going away any time soon. So, I am a young African American girl in a world in which people of color are seen as less than and are not seen for everything we have contributed to the world. I grew up with Mama, who gave us books to read about our history, not about slavery, but about what we gave to the world. I learned about segregation and she talked to us. She said, "You have to understand where you came from

Children With Learning Differences Exploring Artmaking to Address Deficit-Laden Perspectives, pages 25–33
Copyright © 2024 by Information Age Publishing
www.infoagepub.com
All rights of reproduction in any form reserved.

and how their work gave us what we have today . . . and if they didn't do that . . . moving from beneath White people and serving them, where would we still be?"

I chose this social justice issue for my art because it's kinda like a moral thing. I see all these Black boys being shot and killed and not being given the same justice as a White person. Like the Central Park 5 (see https://people.com/crime/the-central-park-five-where-they-are-now/) and they were brutally beaten . . . and they were told they were guilty even though they weren't. They were grabbed off the street by the police. The boys didn't even know each other. They were accused of rape, and now, they were let out, but the police didn't want to admit they made a mistake. The youngest was about my age. They weren't allowed to know their rights or call someone and they were beaten, brutally beaten by the police. My Mama called me downstairs and explained all of this to me. She had me watch the documentary about it. It is very upsetting. She talks to us when there is something big or major happening. She gives me books on injustices as well as biographies.

I need to know where I came from.

If I don't know my history, then I won't know about me or the people who sacrificed their lives or how to do something about the future so all of this stops. Racism is more intensified now. I am bringing attention to racism. My art addresses it and makes it less of an uncomfortable topic.

If I don't use this art to make a change, then it's going to keep happening and that's not okay. My teachers were proud of me for getting my art in a public gallery. Two teachers came to the exhibition. A guidance counselor said my art took a lot of courage and she was proud of me, but none of the principals said anything to me. My teachers, they have been supportive. The head of the school talked to me. I drew something for him and he came to me and congratulated me, but we didn't talk about what I did or what I said. I don't know if I can have a conversation, because I have social anxiety. I clam up and I can't think. I think the head of upper and lower school would understand the power of my art because he was treated horribly because he learned differently than everyone else. He was discriminated against so I think he would understand. Even though I have social anxiety, I think my art can speak for itself. Someone who came to the gallery loved the way I portrayed the message and was about to cry because it was so powerful.

I never had my social justice art showcased like I did now, but I did quick sketches of social justice art for years. Like, there is a girl half and half. On one side, the girl is White and smiling and thinking "life is good" and "I don't have to do anything because my life is easy." And the Black girl on the other side has tears on her face and tape across her mouth with a smiley face drawn over it . . . and that symbolizes how White people think "they are fine" and "they don't need a say" and Black people should just be happy not having a voice. And the Black girl is crying because she is saying, "I have all these situations I have to deal with and the White girl doesn't." I did another doodle of a Black girl's hair and in cursive I wrote the words "nasty and nappy" and other words I am not going to say because they are offensive. I did another one too, but it wasn't very big. It was a portrait of a Black girl's face. It's not finished. The teacher put it up before I finished it, but she didn't know. There are cut out hands all around the drawing that frame the picture. You can see the girl's face and the statement, "Don't touch my hair." I never heard anything about what the art meant to people. I get compliments on it like "that looks nice," but nothing ever deep. It would have been a great opportunity to talk about this, but no one ever asked or talked about it.

The reason I do this social justice art is because I want them to know that kids know about what's going on in the world. When they leave, we don't want this to smack them in the face. I think the school does a good job talking about things going outside of school, but when it comes to racism or discrimination, we can do better. We are talking about intelligence and about what we are worth and I think we could use that to talk about what's going on in the world out there. Since my art, a student started a group. A group of kids could get together and talk about injustice and brutality and it wasn't all Black kids. It was very diverse.

I want my voice to be heard. My teachers support me and let me learn about Black people. But what's not happening is taking what I am learning, which I think everyone should know, and they learn too. I am not sure why, but maybe because it doesn't affect them. Most of my teachers—but two—are White. That—racism—doesn't really affect them. They don't have to fight for what they have. They are just given things and that's privilege. We are not less than. We are not less important. We are important. I can only do my best to bring this to their attention, because if I do more, they might think I am overstepping boundaries. If I press too hard, am I trying to teach them how to teach? They might think so. The school took out history, but really? I get it, college is important and we are learning about learning strategies, but I wanted to learn in the history class. And now, I am in the 10th grade, and they took history away for my grade. I have to wait until next year. I want to show people what really happened. All people to know children, adults, and just people were arrested and killed for believing they mattered, that they had rights. That would be like erasing the Holocaust. It happened. You can't pretend it didn't. Hitler did horrendous things. And here, the civil rights movement still matters. You are being challenged. We need to understand the struggle and how far we have come and how far we have to go. And we have so much work to do. We lost Malcom X, those four little girls in the church bombing, Martin Luther King Jr., Emmet Till, Jimmy Lee Jackson, Medgar Evans, and too many to name. They kill to silence, and yet we are still standing.

This school did the Dear Martin project and it made me happy inside. I am bringing my culture into the world even though the world hates us, hates it, since we were brought overseas.

And then there is the injustice in our government. White people here say racism doesn't happen now or racial injustice, but it does. It's like they want to avoid it. They whisper about it as though it should not be spoken or stay hidden.

My Mama will take what I learn and what I know and encourage me to use my art to express my thoughts. When my Mama saw my artmaking. She was shocked. She thought it was deep. She wants me to use it in college and use it to help others. I want to make a difference. I want to have enough influence and build it up over time and share my art. I want people to see things differently and realize, "Wow! I never thought of anything like that before." I want them to do something, say something. When you see racial discrimination happening, then say something. Don't just sit there. It's not going away. And if you think it's happening, then it is probably happening. Do something.

I started this art by thinking of myself and my experiences as a Black female. I started by looking at images about justice and race. I saw a lot of Martin Luther King Jr., Trevon Martin, Malcolm X, and a lot of people with silhouettes. But the Trevon Martin photo caught my eye. It was a picture of him next to the person who killed him. And something told me that I should do my art on the unfair justice system.I saw kids who were killed for being Black. I wanted people to know justice is blind. How can you justify a lynching?

Figure 4.1 Injustice.

Social Justice Issue: There are so many racist issues going on that it is hard for me as a Black woman to get by in the world built up by the dominant race of White people.

Social Justice Stance: Schools need to educate the students about "our" history—meaning everyone's history whether you are Black, White, Purple, or Brown.

There is so much to talk about, but I will begin here with this list I looked up:

Tamir Rice

Trayvon Martin

Michael Brown

Emmit Till

Cameron Tillman

VonDerrit Myers Jr.

Laquan McDonald

Carey Smith-Viramontes

Jeffrey Holden

Qusean Whitten

What do these names have in common? They were all killed by police, except for Emmet Till, who was killed by a White mob for whistling at a White woman. It is heartbreaking to me to know this. And the real fact, he didn't even whistle at this White woman. It was all a lie! She lied about him! Emmet Till was just a kid . . . murdered . . . tortured . . . because he was Black. And being Black, well, that wasn't going to be accepted. And because he was Black . . . because of the color of his skin . . . he was murdered . . . kidnapped . . . dumped in a river with a weight on him to make sure he sank to the bottom . . . beaten . . . died . . . died alone.

And when I think about this, I can't change my race. I cannot wipe my skin color off. It's on my face. I am judged. I don't get a chance. I am judged the moment White people see me. They might think we are all drug addicts or we are going to shoot everyone up or I might steal from you or I am going to harm you in some way . . . and it's all because of the color of my skin? I don't get the privilege you get if you are White. I can't hide behind my skin color.

I grew up in a White suburban area. All the Black kids think I am too White. They get mad at me because I am too privileged. To be Black, it means, I guess, they think I am privileged. That glass ceiling is made of brick. I am Black and female and privileged. And when I am with White kids, they think I am too Black. They think I am ghetto or my hair...they just don't get I can't be out in the rain. It's going to get nappy and they say it is too kinky and I get too Black and they want me to talk proper and to talk Black means to talk slang...the only difference between me and the White people is that God made me Brown. I love me, but the world tells me something different. I love my brown eyes, my lips, my skin, and my hair. I have been called an Oreo...by both Black and White kids...you know, Black on the outside and White on the inside. So going to school with White kids and White teachers, because I never had a Black teacher, I don't learn anything about being Black. I can't wear my hair in a low ponytail like White girls, because it will break off. I go to school and live with White people and sometimes I resent my mom for raising me in the suburbs. Sometimes I wish I was with my people. Maybe I should have been raised in a city. Maybe I should have been raised around more people who look like me. I am looked down on because I am privileged. It's like Black people think I am spoiled.

I think I would love myself more if I was with other Black people. I would have loved myself more. I think I wouldn't be depressed. I would embrace my ethnicity. I would embrace me. I don't see a lot of things that look like me. And I don't learn about my people in school. I don't learn anything about my people. In my English class, I did a presentation every day for Black History Month, but when the month was over, that was it. It was the end of the discussion. Every day I talked about someone who made a difference and paved the way.

And then for Pride month, everyone did something. When I say that, I mean White people. And I felt invisible. I am beautiful. It is part of my insecurity. I am beautiful. It is a struggle for me to love myself. It is a struggle when the world doesn't seem to love you and you don't fit in. I am either not Black enough or I am too White.

Schools need to teach more about Black people. There are White kids in our school using the "n" word. It's not okay for him to use that word. It's not okay for Black people to use that word. You can't say "White trash" or "dirty Jew" or "cracker" so why is it okay for White kids at my school to use that word? It's a terrible word and it means savage and animal . . . and it should not be used in or out of school. I know rappers use it, but it's not okay. I don't agree with the word.

Teach us about our history. If it weren't for the civil rights movement, I wouldn't even be here at this school. Slavery had an impact on our country and people finally figured out it was wrong, but we are still paying for it today. Black scholars, such as Carter Woodson and W. E. B. Du Bois, learned that the only way to free Black people from being shamed about their origins was to teach them the actual history that textbooks leave out. Textbooks come from Texas and they make decisions about what we learn? When we learn who we are in school, we are visible. We matter.

Don't think it's true? Just 3 days ago, in a White suburb, the police got involved in a racial incident in school. White students were making racially offensive comments and a Black student walked in. The student wasn't allowed to leave. I played softball for this White town. The girls were sweet. I was the only Black person on that team. It surprised me what happened. But just to make sure you understand, it happens everywhere. Up north people don't say it to your face, but they show it. In the south, they say it. They say it out loud. My sister had Asian girls tell her they don't play with Black girls. My sister was in tears. It made me very angry to hear that happened. I don't want to talk about what people have said to me. It's too hurtful.

My Artmaking

The blindfold-flag on the girl is representing that justice in America is blind no matter how much you try to change it. The noose in the background brings attention to all of the lynchings that have gone on in the United States of America. This whole piece is showing how the law is unfair to the American community and how justice for us isn't as clear as it is justice for White people. At the bottom the gravestones are showing all of the people who have sacrificed themselves for freedom only to have a noose dangling over their final resting place.

Advice, If You are Interested

I want people to have a more open mind and realize we need to address this now. Standing there isn't going to work. You gotta say something. You gotta do something. You can't say this isn't happening. Say something. Do something. It is your business. It's everyone's business because we all matter.

What if you saved someone's life? What if you stopped something worse from happening? You have a responsibility. What if they wanted to harm themselves because they hate themselves? That's not right. It's evil. Those words or those thoughts come from nothing good.

You have to do something.
We all do.
You can't just walk away because you are White and
those things are supposedly not your business.
It is your business.
Make it your business.
Show that you care.
Do something.

I hope my art inspires you to take a stand. I hope you choose to say something if you hear someone make a racist comment...or something that puts someone down. Stand up. Do something. Take a stand. I did. I used my art. What will you do?

5

Learning "Dis-ability"

Hunter Langan

This was extremely unique. I wasn't expecting this. I didn't expect this in an art class let alone in another class. I do my best, but to put something in my art and knowing my brother and other people can benefit or learn from this, that was great. It was like a boulder off my chest. To express how I feel about this was amazing. I am so much more confident in myself and my learning difference. I didn't have to hold this in any longer. For years, I held back. Well, all my life. That's sad. Now, I see things in a new light.

To share what I have experienced and to have them hear me, to actually hear me was great. I am not used to people listening to me. I am

Children With Learning Differences Exploring Artmaking to Address Deficit-Laden Perspectives, pages 35–44
Copyright © 2024 by Information Age Publishing
www.infoagepub.com

not a leader. I like to be in the background, but people encourage me to be a leader. From my basketball church and I have letters from this Christian school, but they didn't treat me like that, but he said, "Not to be afraid to be a leader because God chose you to be one." I keep that on my bedpost and my mother brought it up and I have kept it up ever since. I think my mom may have brought that up because I think I needed to be inspired. I think she felt it was time for me to see how other people see me. She always does little things like that and I love it. I am very appreciative of them. I don't always feel so good about me. I think sometimes I need to feel better about myself. I am competing with others, but really, I am competing with myself. I always feel like I need to change. I am humble. I don't compliment myself and I don't like to be outspoken. My actions tell people how much I care and what matters to me.

In my art, I was outspoken. I was out of my comfort zone. I was stepping out. At first, I was doing it for other people. But then, I realized I needed and wanted to do it for me. I am always thinking about the person behind me to help ... everywhere ... literally. I help them before I help myself. In most of my life, I help other people no matter what. I do this for everything. Literally, like, I work at a vitamin company. I always walk around the counter and open the door for every customer because I am so passionate about what I do. I wanted to do that. I always hold the door. It's a way to humble myself. I want everyone to know we are the same. We are equal. And I think all people deserve the same treatment, you know, the way you would like to be treated.

It's iffy, you know. I can see my brother do it sometimes for me. I try to show him how to respect and thank my mom for a meal before we eat. I see my friends not thank their moms and they just start eating, but I don't. I say thank you first. I feel like my mom and dad raised me to be a good gentleman for everybody. I don't hold a grudge to my teachers who put me down. They think they are better than me, but I still show respect. I try not to believe they are better than me. It used to get to me, but ever since I got to this school, I feel I have grown up. I grew up into who I am. It's a flower bloom. I am treated with respect here. I am not called dumb by teachers here. It's hard to look up to someone when you are called names. I still showed them respect, but they called me out of my name. It still sticks with me. It hurts. They have an opinion, but it doesn't define my actions or who I am today. It all left away.

When I did this social justice art, this was the first step of stepping out, of speaking out. I have dyslexia and I am not blaming my dyslexia for mistakes. I normally hold things in. And by that, I don't always show my feelings. I am very calm. I like things calm. I don't want to have pointless arguments. I don't say when things bother me. I keep it inside. I don't say it. It's very hard for me. Even with my parents, I don't say things. Our family is close. We are so close. Everything we do is together. When my dad was hurt, we all hurt. I don't want to hurt them if I tell them how I feel. If it is difficult, I never share it. But with this art, I let something out that I kept inside my whole life. I didn't think anyone would change, so why bother. They are adults.

I never looked at art this way. I didn't get to do this art before. I could see it and feel it. It was a wow for me. I didn't realize that art could be so meaningful. I never realized a picture could be seen a thousand ways and how deep it could go . . . I was just trying to get dyslexia out there and I was hoping they wanted to know more. It's not a sob story, but I want to share what I experienced because there are other kids too . . . and there are kids are just as silent as me or more silent or they are struggling. Do you know who is struggling? Just because kids are quiet doesn't mean everything is okay. And I don't think people realize this. And maybe people laugh or show other emotions, but inside they are hurting.

My brother and I struggle with dyslexia, so I did my art for him. This is a learning difference, not a "dis-ability." We learn. We're smart. It's not that we are unable to learn. It's that we *are* able to learn. I decided to put my face right up front because I wanted people to know. My dad and my brother struggle with it and all of my cousins. My uncle also has dyslexia and he turned to art and became an artist and now he makes a living being an artist. I made my face two halves. I wanted to get more writing in my art. I wanted the most important parts of my details about me, like a thesis. I wanted to catch their eyes. I wanted them to read what I think is super important and what I think should be done. I wanted to put words with my face. I made the background silver and grey because that's the national dyslexia color. I read about this on the web. I wanted to put the stat that 1 out of 10 people have dyslexia.

Most people don't even realize they have it. It can range from mild to severe. When I put the letters on my art, I wanted them to see what I see. I want you to struggle the way I struggle. What would you have done with that? A lot of people have anxiety when they have dyslexia, so I cut out these letters and placed them in the right place, just like a spell check on art. My dad switches his D's and I wanted you to experience that. I did a spell check on my own with my art. My face is cut in two. These were representing how my thoughts were kept to myself and most people don't see that I experienced this or that I felt that way. So, I used my art to show what I kept inside and now, I am showing it to everyone. It was kinda scary. I do like to keep a lot of things to myself, but I knew I was in the right hands. I felt safe. I trusted Christa and the process. I wrote what I felt. No limits. I made art that reflected my thoughts. Again, no limits. She was there to support me throughout this process. It meant a lot to me. I would not have done this if I didn't feel safe or didn't trust or didn't feel like someone understood me . . . or looked at me like a failure . . . I don't want people to judge me or blame me . . . I needed to feel comfortable first . . . I needed to know it was okay . . . I looked into this on my free time and I realized how many people do struggle with this and there are so many books about it . . . I learned I wasn't alone. I had a group to support me. My brother liked this. He is a crazy little fellow and it was for him, not just me. My brother experienced the same thing and I learned that it was worse for him. The teachers treated him poorly. They would say he wasn't smart and they would focus on other kids. So, I wanted you to know what it's like to be in my brain. Letters and numbers float around and flow around in my thoughts.

My teachers, however, did not understand this whatsoever. I don't blame them. I still look up to them and respect them. It does kinda suck, but I still respect them because that's how I was raised.

When I look at my art, I feel good. I feel really good. I expressed myself. I shared what happened to me so I could help other students and teachers. I want students to know they are smart. They matter. They have so much to offer. And no matter what, there is no such thing as a disability. We are capable of learning. It's just that we learn differently. Why is this so hard for people to understand. My art has meaning. My words matter. And hopefully, it helps somebody. Remember this: You are not alone. I am standing there with you.

I wanted to do something 3D and I decided to step outside of my comfort zone. This time, I did 2D and it felt good to try something new from my art teacher. She helped me with the varnish and made it super-duper shiny. We talked about what I could do and talked about it. We worked together.

Figure 5.1 Learning "sis-ability."

Here is my abstract from the social justice art exhibition:

Social Justice Issue: Public schools do a horrible job with people with learning differences.

Social Justice Stance: Public schools need to help more with students with learning differences.

I was treated like crap. I was treated differently in school. I was happy that eighth grade was there. They didn't have a high school. The school literally gave up on me. Basically, they would take me out of class, but like, the things they were making me do were like multiple times tables. It was just like a time killer. They thought I didn't have a purpose sort of thing. I was taken out of class for this. I was the only person in my grade that had to do this. I felt like it was sort of left out. I felt really different. I felt like they didn't care about my education or learning or learning about me in general. I was like on the basketball team and that. My friends had respect for me. They noticed I was treated horribly. And as a kid, that's crazy. The school treated me horribly. From first grade up through eighth grade. I mean literally, it was everyone. I was 5 years old and didn't know schools like the one I am at exist. How could I? I was only just a kid. It was *every* teacher, literally, every teacher who treated me like crap. I expected to see some nice teachers. They targeted me. I needed to receive the help, but they thought less of me. I could literally not learn if they didn't believe in me. They didn't teach me. They just gave me worksheets to do to take up time. They thought I was less than. Honestly, I literally and honestly cannot tell you one thing that I learned in eighth grade. What I learned there was nothing. I have been here for 4 years and I have learned so much.

Here, teachers pay attention to it. They care about you personally and your schoolwork too. They care about the work. And when people care, then that motivates me to do my work. I cannot think of a time I failed anything here. I failed at my other school. They didn't think I could do anything. They thought less of me. And when someone thinks less of me, why should I try? Why should I learn from you?

I am out of my comfort zone right now, and this has been amazing. I never spoke of this before now. I am from a tight and close family, and they didn't know about this. They do now. It feels good because I have been holding this in for 18 years. It's been a long time coming. I thought this would be a perfect way to let my parents know what I have been through. I don't want them to be scared. There are better things to come and I want other students to know that.

When I researched how many students have learning differences, the first thing I noticed was the word disability appears. I made a face. I completely disagreed with that. I am literally like everyone else. I am not my learning difference. We all have differences. I can carry a conversation like anyone else, just like a normal human being. I don't like to say it, but the word disability is like saying "I am dumb"... "he can't grow out of that"... "get out"... "you can't learn"... so, it's just like being at my old school. Just saying the word makes me sad. I can't believe that word is still used. I hate saying that word. It brings people down. I don't like to do that. I don't want it to be done to me. I want the same fairness back. In 2017–2018, the number of students between PreK and college who received special education services was around 14% or 7 million kids. So, I thought, being in my own shoes, with my experience, "How many kids are neglected right now?" How many more kids are not getting the services they need. I can only imagine what it is like to be in a public school and not get the services you need.

To this day, I am still afraid to raise my hand. I am afraid of saying the wrong thing. I tend to be quiet. And they literally did damage to me. I realize there are still good adults out there, but when you are told to look up to these adults, that's scary. Do they really treat kids like this? Do they think I am not smart? Doing this work, and being a senior, I am regaining my confidence. I realize I wasn't going to be judged. I felt that throughout this art. They understand. There are people who understand me. That felt great. It feels like a millionaire dollars! It builds up confidence! I am not afraid to ask questions when I feel this way.

I learned that kids are bullied in school for having a learning difference. But I was not bullied by kids. I was bullied by the teachers. That is sort of crazy to think about. I think that kids might be bullied because you are different than someone and that might be why kids pick on other kids, but to have adults do the same thing is just crazy to think about. I was fairly quiet about it. Looking back, I wish I said something. Now that I am older, I have learned to speak up. And when you are in the situation, I was the "dumb one" so why should I listen to him? It was so difficult. A teacher literally said to me, "You should just drop out of school . . . there is no point." My mom went there and they told my mom, "He is not going to amount to much." This was said in a religious school. They are supposed to be there for students. It is said in service, but we don't have to be there for kids. My parents didn't even know. I thought it was better for me to take it on. I didn't want them to worry. I took it on. I was too scared. That was what it was like to be bullied. To speak up to a teacher? That's not going to happen. We don't have a voice. The teachers are treated like kings and we are less. We don't have a voice.

In this art, I feel I have a voice. I have been through a lot. This is the first time I have ever talked about this. My parents don't even know. This is the *first* time I ever opened up. It's powerful. It means something to me. I want my parents to be satisfied that I am in a better position now. I don't want them to worry about me. I got this now. I am going to prove those horrible teachers wrong. They thought they could win. They did not. I am going to college. I am successful in school. I like being able to prove them wrong. I cannot wait for my parents to see this. This is very *powerful!* My grandparents are coming too! This means something! And my cousin is coming too! He is an artist and very good at what he does.

I want to make a difference with my art and my story. I hope people realize that if you are struggling at school, you are *not* dumb! You just need extra help and that's fine. Just stick to it and hopefully, my story gives you motivation if you are struggling. I am hoping that when I graduate from college, I am coming back to tell the teachers that they actually helped me. Their bullying motivated me in the end. It was wrong, but I looked at it differently. I am hoping this leaves a good message.

Outside of Art

I am the sports guy. I don't do art outside of art. It keeps me calm. I have a super stressful course and then I go to art and calm down. And especially after physics, that's stressful. I started doing art at my old school, but I wasn't really taught well. We all had to do the same thing and we were taught by a video projected on the wall. We watched it and then we did what she did on the video. And we all did the same thing and weren't allowed to have an opinion. And then, we were given a grade. How do you get a grade? It was really weird. But when I came here, I took a bunch of art classes and I really do enjoy it.

I don't do art in any other classes like history, English, science, or math classes. I only do art in art class. Maybe teachers don't want us to do art to keep us all together on the same level? Maybe other students wouldn't like it, but it would be really cool to have it in my other classes. You could throw off ideas in chemistry or in math or in history. I am not sure teachers know how to do this.

I would want social justice in schools for everyone to have. I learned a lot through other people and listening to what they experienced. They learned I had dyslexia and I learned so much about them. I didn't know Mohammad Ali had it. I learned so much and I didn't feel alone. Maybe students wouldn't feel alone either if they knew other people thought about this too. Are there any schools that do this work every semester? I didn't find anything that told me this was something that happened in schools. This was so rare. I think I found one school and then there were a few around the world. That's it.

I would want them to also do art. I don't mean you have to do it in every class, but I would want students to do this work. It helps you think outside the box. That's how school should be. It should be opening your eyes. It should be helping you see something bigger. I like that I can express myself freely and it is actually easier to take paint or create instead of writing it or reading about it. There is no right or wrong in art. In class, you either get the answer right or wrong, but not in art. I like the concept of having done my art and how meaningful all of this was to me. And this way, you can tell your teacher what you learned and what's important to you.

I think this changed me. I am really different. From the research I did, I am a different person. I feel better. It feels good, I guess. I am not alone. I am not the only one struggling. Since I have done this piece, I am talking about it and I shared it. I talked with my dad about dyslexia and he told me how he was treated and that opened my eyes up. They were brutal to him. It was like the "r" word and a teacher called him that. I can't imagine how that brought my dad down. It opened up talking with my dad. I didn't expect that. My dad was extremely grateful I did this. We look and act the same. I wish I had a photo to show you. I also talked with my mom and she is very understandable. I think my mom fights for me and my brother and wants to make sure I have rights. I have not had a chance to talk to as many students as I would like, but I did share this with my teachers. My teachers were crying. I realized they were moved. They wanted to make sure they never treat a student like that and I assured them they did not. I am interested in helping other students. I would like to make my own school some-day...maybe I could do that. I want to take more art classes and see what happens. This work has made me a different person. I am stronger. I feel empowered. I know I can make a difference. I never thought my art would have the impact it has had. I want to keep doing this work. Everyone should have this chance. Everyone.

6

Make or Break

Madison Gould

I never thought I would ever be a published author. I never thought my art would be in a real gallery. I mean, it's just, I never thought that what I did was ever that significant or worthy or even worthy enough to be in a book. I matter. This is what I learned. My voice matters. This is what I learned. And, my art has purpose. It can make a difference and say things my words do not.

This is amazing! It makes me smile. I love being able to say, "I am in a book and what I do matters." I like knowing I am letting them know my voice matters. I like to do the unthinkable, the unimaginable.

Children With Learning Differences Exploring Artmaking to Address Deficit-Laden Perspectives, pages 45–55
Copyright © 2024 by Information Age Publishing
www.infoagepub.com

I wrote this when I thought about this art I made:

I just thought I was like every other kid.
I struggle.
Everyone struggles,
has their quirks,
and have their issues.
I never thought someone would ever want to hear about what I thought.
It's important.
It's not gibberish.
It's my life.

When I think about my art, and what matters, the day I went to see my art at the gallery, it was a stressful day, everyone was on edge in my family. I remember going into that room, I went off on my own and read what other artists created. My parents didn't look around that much. They were fixated on my piece and couldn't stop looking at it. The arguments that were had just evaporated. Everyone went from anger to a pure softness of empathy. What I wrote made my Nana and Papa Choo cry (We call him this because he likes trains). He couldn't read, because he needed his glasses, so my Nana read my words to him.

My Mom was silent. She spoke very little after reading about my art. My Nana came to me and told me that she never realized how bad it was for me back then... not until I put my thoughts on paper and made my art into a story.

Everything went quiet with everyone. I couldn't believe it. That morning was tough and to see the power my art could have... that it could influence people and their emotions with one another... that sometimes words can just have more effect than we are aware of... that just a few words can change everything. I didn't realize my art would have such an effect, especially on adults. I remember my Nana came to me crying after seeing my art and reading about it. She asked for a copy of my abstract because it had so much meaning to her. If my art and my voice can inspire others, then I want to continue my work.

I saw my art affect people and it happened right before me. I realized then, I want to use my art to give back. I want to show people what

I can make of myself. It's my life's work and if this is how I can do it or if this is my calling, then I am going to do it.

My art is personal. I don't blame my family for anything that has happened to me in the past in any way shape or form. Having a child with differences, whether it be mental or physical, can be hard for anyone to understand. I didn't even understand myself back then. It was hard for my family to be on the same page. Everyone did everything they could do to get me in a happy environment. Whether it was at home or at school, they always wished me happiness. No matter what happened, I want them to know that all has been forgiven. I love my life now. My family needed to hear that. I don't have hatred in my heart. I forgave.

My injustice is not like everyone else's problems. My problems are not other people's issues. And what I lived may not be as traumatic as someone else's, but it is my life, and I don't need to compare it to anyone. Instead, I need to share it. And although I do compare my life to other people a lot, I shouldn't.

In my head, when I think about my art, a part of me says I shouldn't say all of this and let all this out in public. But what I learned was that I feel I can loosen up a little and use art to do that. I trust what's happening. With the art and writing and thinking, I am raw right now. I am a little scared because this can go either way. I can be accepted for me or I can be rejected. But what's most important to know is that my art, it's me.

I wrote this poem when thinking about what this art means to me:

This is me.
This art is me.
I am exposing myself.
I am exposing me.
I am coming apart on to this very page.
I needed to let my story out.

My art began with a silhouette. The silhouette represents me. The cracks are me breaking and coming apart. I am opening up and sharing my story. I am being confident. And, I am using my inner strength to tell my story through art, and then, I let it go. I need to let it go in my art.

I see my art as all of my stories together in my silhouette, and then, all of these broken pieces come off of me, but they are me. This art is me. I am coming together, making me, and this is my story. These pieces are parts of my story. They are my experiences. These are my thoughts, feelings, and expressions.

Throughout my art, I was in a more vulnerable state. It is not easy to come out like this through your art, but I did it. Whether it be my story about me or my beliefs or what I think as a person, it's about me. I wondered, "Will they judge me? Will I be criticized?"

I was in a vulnerable state when I processed my thoughts and translated them into my art.

I am in the raw.

I am fragile

I like parts of me can shatter

And then,

I am whole

My fear . . .

I don't want people to judge me

Will people think my story doesn't matter?

People have it worse, right?

And I know this wholeheartedly,

and it's somewhat ludicrous to think that my voice matters,

that my story matters,

But I learned,

It does.

My life influenced my art, and of course, my story. I share my story with you so you can better understand my art and my message. I have an upper middle-class family and I get everything I could possibly need materialistically. All is provided to me, but is my life something people want to read, to look at through my art?

I am not saying that I am not grateful for everything I have. I am grateful for everything my parents have done and provided me with. I know I am spoiled. I get what I need just by asking, and that's the materialistic need being met. But emotionally, it doesn't always feel the same. At school, at home, or in the world, that's not always the case. I question whether I am worth it.

Self-doubt is a huge struggle for me. I know there are people who have it a million or billion more times worse than me, and that makes me think I have no reason to be sad, because my problems seem insignificant. When I think about people who do not have food or water, I am here talking about needing emotional attentiveness. And I realize I should not compare myself to other people, so I wonder, "Is that complaining? Or is this more importantly, my lack of self-worth?" I have always had a difficult time loving myself. At times I will see myself in a brighter light, but it is only temporary. Then the criticism comes in and this other voice tells me I am not important and that I am not good enough . . . that I am not enough . . . I always do my best . . . and then my best isn't good enough . . . I tell myself I don't struggle with self-appearance . . . This is me mentally being broken . . . not stable . . . I struggle with mild depression and it effects my day-to-day life . . . the mind is a dangerous place to me . . . I have anxiety attacks . . . I can't help it . . . it becomes a storm and I drown in these negative thoughts . . . when I picture glass breaking, it flies up in the air . . . this is a blow to my head . . . to my mentality . . . to my thoughts . . . it's a blow . . . things that were good or bad . . . dyslexia . . . ADHD . . . depression . . . anxiety . . . If I didn't have these things happen in my life . . . I can't take these pieces and not make them a part of me . . . I can't imagine these things not being with me.

In the picture it shows that I am broken. It shows that I am looking upward . . . looking at something. I am looking for help. I am looking for a hand to piece me back together. My Mom, Nana, and Papa Choo. They have been there for me for the most emotional time in my life. Those three people have been there for me to support me, to coach me, to encourage me . . . to be present . . . to listen . . . and to bring me back, to bring my pieces back . . . that my emotional health matters . . . that I matter . . . that what I feel and think matters. This piece represents me frozen in time. It represents a part of my life at that moment. I was feeling that I was struggling the most. The reason why these pieces are falling away from me is because I'm losing sight of the bigger picture of my life. I am mentally struggling. I can't comprehend my own life . . . this picture is what I fear most, "Where are the hands that will lend me the help I need?" They are gone. I am alone. I am afraid of losing the people who piece me back together. Those people help me see the bigger picture of my life and show me that there is meaning in life. I don't feel like I am capable of putting myself back together.

Knowing that I can lose my mom, Nana, or my Papa Choo is anxiety ridden. It takes a mental toll on me. I can't help but cry, but it is inevitable. Everyone has to deal with this fear...Depression. It's one of the worst mental illnesses I have seen and experienced. It's nasty and it's horrible. It has almost taken the lives of a few of my friends. At one point, I thought of taking my own life because of my depression. I remember listening to the lyrics in middle school. It was Bohemian Rhapsody. I remember listening to the lyrics he said, "I don't want to die, but I sometimes wish I had never been born at all." That had an impact on me. I was afraid of death, but at the same time I welcomed it, I didn't want to experience losing any of my loved ones and I didn't want to experience the overwhelming sadness. So, I thought it would be better to take my life rather than experiencing it all over again. At a young age I lost my sister to a heart disease and I have never experienced such sadness and I didn't want to relive it. I remember I talked about this with my mom. None of us got to see my sister live her full life. We never got to see her grow up. I often think to myself how different life would be if she was still here. And all the fun wonderful experiences of life she gets to endure alongside me. What would life be like when she first goes into high school, or goes to her first school dance, or when she goes to her dream college to pursue her dreams, or maybe even one day seeing her get married...but she is gone. And who was I to end my own life and take that away from the ones I loved. And the reason why I came to this conclusion was because of an old friend. He told me that I have a family that loves me and he told me that would be selfish of me to do such a thing, because there are so many people who love me, want to be around me, love being with me every day, and he said I would cause so much pain if you were to just throw that away. When he said the word selfish it felt like a slap to the face. It was as if I was in a whole other world, his words were sobering to me. I would never wish to cause pain or be selfish towards the ones I love. It's not in my nature. I like to think of myself as a giving person. I would give the clothes off my back just to make someone I love happy. And I took a step back. I realized this wasn't me. Hearing that I would be selfish, I was being reckless. I was only still a kid. I was still developing. Change is coming. And it's going to be for the better, even though it didn't seem like it at the moment. There was no point in me ending what I had. I needed to keep growing and developing as a person. When I was in that stage, I was really, honestly, I think I was just looking for people to tell me it would be okay... but now, sympathy only made it worse. It was a slap of reality. It made me realize that I wasn't thinking straight and I needed that.

I was thinking about this the other day. In my life, I am surrounded by two different kinds of people. One is, life is hard and you need to suck it up and deal with it. The other tells me life is going to be okay. And that is what makes me strong. I need both and I need a balance. I sometimes need a slap of reality to help me get my head back in place. I need to keep my mind on what is most important. And both of those perspectives make me whole again. If I got one side more than the other, if I had more reassurance or comfort, then I think I might give up in life. I might be a lazy person. Or if I got too strict, I might be a hard ass, I guess. But both of those perspectives shape my morals and personality and me.

I would take being loved over having a big house or things. I will pick people to love me and to be surrounded by love over anything with money. This is something I have been learning all of my life.

I know someone struggling with this whether she wants love or money to support people she cares about, but what's most important is love. It's a priority. She has been there for me even when times were tough for her. I want this woman to know I look up to her very much. She opens up to me like nobody else does and she truly understands me. Love or money, but when it comes down to picking a partner or a friend, you should go with the people who are going to ride alongside of you to the very end and treat you as an equal. I just want this woman to know I love her very much. I always tell her this. I tell her this every day. She is the one that inspires me every day to be the person that I am. And she gets me through everything, every little thing. She is always welcome to come to me and I cherish our relationship more than life. I don't know where I would be without this woman. She takes my fears and shows me that I need to enjoy what I have while I have it for as long as I can and to not take anything for granted. I am dedicating this chapter to her and people like her. I am accepted. I am loved. She is one of those pieces coming from my art. She is one of the biggest pieces of my life. There is a song called "You're the Biggest Part of Me." It's so true. She is the biggest part of me.

To conclude this chapter I just want you the reader to know that mental health matters. Whether you are dealing with it or witnessing it, you need to know that you matter. Take some time to step back and take a look at your life and see the bigger picture. Look at your life and rejoice. Live your life to the best of your ability while maintaining yourself.

Title: Make or Break

Social Justice Issue: Mental Health Awareness

Social Justice Stance: Mental illness is real and impacts our society both physically and figuratively.

Figure 6.1 Make or break.

I am interested in this topic because I have been told I have a few mental diagnoses such as mild depression and anxiety. I also have two learning differences which are dyslexia and ADD (attention deficit disorder). A lot of stuff happened in my childhood, which brought all of this into my life. I was 5 years old. I lost my sister. I also couldn't understand the words I was reading. Losing a family member and struggling in school really hit me hard. I had panic attacks and school was always bombarding me with, "Why are you doing things this way?" and questioning and criticizing me...and I felt alone...and I didn't like who I was. I wanted to be somebody else. And since then, I have always had that mild depression and anxiety. I didn't know until recently because no one ever told me. I just found out a few weeks ago. Why? Because I am now closer to being an adult. The feelings I was feeling made more sense when I knew. I didn't know why I felt sad for no reason. And now it makes more sense. And now this gives me more closure and what other kids are faced with too. I didn't see my therapist for a long time because I didn't feel I needed anybody. I just felt like she wasn't actually listening. It was pointless to go. I went to see her now because I figured that's how I felt back then and now that I see her, I realize I have what I have and it was one of the best things I have ever done. My mom just found her and said she would take me to this person and that's how I met her. Now that I know, it was definitely impactful and insightful for me. It opened my eyes to a lot of different things. I was a little shocked, but I wasn't surprised. Everything clicked. I even thought about it after. I thought for hours. I realized why I felt this way, why I felt alone all the time, and it changed the way I thought.

Nobody comforted me when I lost my sister. People said I talked about it too much and said it was annoying. But I was grieving, and kids would roll their eyes. The teachers didn't do much. They didn't pay attention. I wasn't one of those kids who was smart enough to function in one of their classes, so they didn't care. Oftentimes, kids would call me "stupid" or "retarded" or "dumb" because I didn't know how to read or write. Kids would make fun of me when I tried my best to do those things in front of me and it was incredibly embarrassing. And sometimes kids would beat me up because I was different and do horrible things like pull my hair, kick me, and tell me I was less and that I would never be part of a functioning classroom. They made me feel like I was never going to be "normal."

I wasn't worth the time.

They kept me in a trailer in the back of the school. I didn't come into the building. I wasn't welcome. I was so isolated. I even spent time in there during recess. The other kids played on the playground at recess. I would watch them from the trailer window. They thought I was too slow, so they put me in a classroom who also had similar issues to mine. Oftentimes, they did individual lessons so I could understand each topic. They would keep me out of recess because they thought if I had more time to practice reading and English, then I would get better. It got to the point where they even kept me after school. I felt very isolated. I felt very left out. I felt out of my grade. I felt like I wasn't like anyone else. I was unnatural. I felt I didn't fit in anywhere. Oftentimes, I would come to school and tell the principal about friends and social situations and things were said, but nothing happened. I didn't really have friends, like one or two, but they left. I experienced this up to fifth grade.

Since coming here, I have been able to meet people who are just like me. I wasn't isolated in a classroom. I felt like I could be more open and grow into my own skin. Nothing held me back anymore. I could do what I wanted. I could make my own story and even though those experiences in the past took a toll on me, they made me who I am now. I feel like I am stronger from those situations. I have a better way of understanding myself and others and I feel like I have accomplished so much since I came here and I would not trade that for anything.

It was definitely life-changing. My art. This process.

I have not shared this before. I have not opened up about my depression until now. It makes me a little anxious. I am a very happy person, but sometimes I have bursts of sadness and I don't want people freaking out. I never went into depth about my anxiety either. It might bring my feelings back and it could break me down. It's kind of hard to talk about it right now because to me that is just a topic that should not be said out loud, but I am saying it now to show that it's okay to be the way I am. My mom always told me that not everybody would understand 'cause it's not something everybody goes through at this age. Kids wouldn't understand my learning differences or my mental differences. And people wouldn't probably accept me for the way I am, but she told me that she loved me exactly the way I am and would not want to change me. And that I should feel confident in myself and realize that my differences make me who I am. She's even opened up to me about her life and how she went through similar things when she grew up so I would know that I am not the only one going through these stages in life. And that it is okay to cry.

This piece is supposed to represent mental health awareness. You never know what someone could be going through. Life is a perplexing thing and it can either make or break you. This piece is a reminder to the world that mental awareness is no figment of our imagination, it is real and is not easy to deal with alone. This piece is me though I may seem broken in this picture, but it is actually me coming back together and becoming the person you see right in front of you right now. I couldn't have pieced myself back together without all of my friends and family, the ones who spent every day loving me, and watching over me every day of my life. Even though life has left many bumps and bruises I wouldn't change a thing.

Conclusion

One main word of advice to teachers and principals is to be open about learning from your students. Not only can they learn from you, but they can teach you too. And if you take the time to listen to one student and invest yourself, you can change a life. We might have learning differences, but that doesn't make us less. It makes us more. We have something to teach . . . to share. Learn from us. And realize that students have lives, thoughts, feelings, and do want to do better. And for kids with mental illnesses, just sitting down and talking with them makes them feel better and makes them feel heard. It might sound so simple, and it is in a way, but students really need this. We need to know we matter to you. We have things going on and sometimes those things might stop us from learning or learning the way you want us to learn. And that our opinion is not inferior. And reaching out to a child doesn't make you seem like you are less than. It will actually make you look like a hero to that child. Just give us a chance. Think about what this art did for me. If you don't know how, then learn. Take a chance. I did. Look what happened. Can you do this for students? Do you believe in us?

7

We Have a Lot to Lose

Alex Sprenger

I just care about how the environment is changing. I get tired of hearing about wildfires and hurricanes and that there are more now than there used to be. I wanted to show what we have and how that impacts us and if we cannot change how we do this, then we won't have our world. I feel sad. I know that making a change in my lifestyle will make a difference, but I am not enough. Even if I am composting, because we compost at the school, it doesn't stop trash from going into the landfills. Sometimes I get angry. And I realize that even though I am trying, I take a car to school . . . I have lights . . . I produce trash . . . I am not perfect. And even if we make changes, it's not enough. All of us

Children With Learning Differences Exploring Artmaking to Address Deficit-Laden Perspectives, pages 57–66
Copyright © 2024 by Information Age Publishing
www.infoagepub.com
57

need to make changes. Governments and companies need to change how they package and use tons of plastic and styrofoam. And maybe instead of having cereal boxes, what would happen if we bring our containers and fill them. It's a change in lifestyle...it's a change in how we work...economics...business...we value materials and owning things...and new gadgets and shoes...and the newness...but how do we change this...it's about psychology...a lot of times, we base our worth by what we have...because we own the newest car, then we are somehow better than our neighbors...or we don't have a lot so we go out and spend money on things so people think we are more like them or just as good.

> *Most of the time*
> *When I feel stressed*
> *I put my phone away*
> *I go to the woods*
> *I go to the waterfall*
> *I just go*
> *I need to break*
> *I need to break away*
> *No emails*
> *No constant messages*
> *Those things stress me out*
> *I need to take a break away*
> *I appreciate what's around me*
> *I appreciate a forest*
> *I have been in one*
> *I appreciate the waterfall*
> *Because I hear the water moving*
> *The wind blows*
> *The leaves crinkle*
> *The trees sway*
> *The birds chirping*
> *The bees fly around me and move onto a flower*
> *I value nature*

We all need a second to be alone and think

Then maybe we would discover our worth is not defined by what we own

But by our relationships

By what we can do to improve ourselves

Our contributions to the world

Our mental health

And maybe then

The shift

How we think

How we feel

Knowing we are connected

Knowing our worth

Then we can help

We can help everything

Even though humans are at the top of the food chain

We don't own the world

We share the world

Everyone has its place

We cannot just take someone's home

We are a community

We are connected

Its coexisting

Recognizing that we have a shared space

A shared world

We will take the time to do something

To help the creatures in this world

Our ocean

Our land

And ultimately,

A world where everything lives in balance

Cherished

Honored

And we are whole again.

First, I just drew a circle and cone. Once I did that, I drew the outline of everything I was going to make. I researched some species affected by climate change: fish, coral, polar bears, orchids, butterflies, and coffee. A lot of things stem from the coral. A lot of things also come from coral bleaching. It gets stressed out and dies. All the fish that rely on the coral, they cannot rely on the coral either. Now, the fish that rely on the coral have nothing to eat. A lot of people make the analogy of Jenga. You can take out some pieces, but then it starts to get unstable and you can't take out too many pieces, then it falls down. It collapses. Every species supports another species in a way just like the Jenga game. They were scattered across the board. I wanted people to know that if we continued to do what we are doing, then they will get lost in space, just like my art. Everything was spread out. I added the oil pastels because they blend very well. It gave a nice space look. It catches the eye more. Color could show what we wouldn't have when it was gone. I tried to show the heat of the sun radiating on the earth. It is a connection to climate change and the greenhouse effect. And then I used colored pencils for the animals. I wanted to show their details. I don't think doing it in Black and White would have done it justice. It was important to see specifics. And the plants were in colored pencil too. I don't think people would care about flowers if they weren't colorful. If I made the art beautiful, then people would see what we are going to lose. The hand and the cone were done with colored pencil too. I wanted it to look clear. I didn't want to get too abstract because I wanted people to understand what I was showing. I want them to interpret my message correctly: If we keep living the way we are, it's not sustainable . . . and we do have a lot to lose.

When I was thinking about this art, I went on Google images. I looked up "Climate Change Art Projects." I found some photos I liked about the earth and art. I liked how the hands were holding the earth. It showed a connection between the hands and the heart. I liked the cracking in the background. It is showing the wear and tear in the environment. The earth was on fire. I don't find joy in that, but it does represent what's happening and sometimes like art doesn't always have to be beautiful. I think when we think of art, we think of beauty. But art is about story. It doesn't need to be a pretty story. Not all books we read have happy endings. The story of our planet isn't heading in the right direction, so it's not "pretty." When I think about social justice and art,

I guess as long as you find a way to symbolize something, it doesn't matter what it looks like. I saw art at the exhibition that was super super simple. One was weight and showed that we need a balance and one life is not more valuable than another. It doesn't need to be intricate. Social justice art is saying what you need to say and get right to it. The art needs to get you thinking. There are multiple ways to do it, but the message stays the same.

This is my art abstract and a photo of my social justice art for the exhibition:

Title: Melting

Social Justice Issue: Humans are living in unsustainable ways that are hindering the life of organisms we share our planet with.

Social Justice Stance: We need government regulations, especially on larger corporations, so they have a cap on the amount of pollutants they are allowed to release. We also need to make changes in our daily lives such as composting, carpooling, and buying less to reduce our carbon footprint.

When I picture our planet, I picture a large home where all life forms share a common place and are provided with life, but recently our home has caught fire. While some of us have been able to change or escape the fire, many have been left in the ashes.

Ever since I was young, I have always been very interested in the topic of environmental sustainability. Our planet is a home for us, but it is also the home of many other living beings. This cause is important because by destroying our home, we are hindering our own ability to live a good life and many other animals. In the freshman year, I joined a program called Global Youth Leadership Institute where I became much more involved with tackling this dilemma. In this program, we traveled to Connecticut, New Mexico, and Costa Rica where we learned how climate change is affecting all of those areas individually. After this, I knew I had to make changes to help our planet.

I wanted to create this art project to help show that the planet is melting onto our hands, and it is our responsibility to change our ways to create a world where all life can live as it used to. I hope that my art can inspire others to see that this issue is a crisis that needs to be talked about. I believe that art has the ability to capture people more than words do.

To create this project, I used a variety of mediums. For the spacey background, I used oil pastels. The melting planet was made with acrylic paint, and the animals and plants were created with colored pencils. I have hope that this social justice art will spark others to think about how their actions may affect our changing planet, and other living creatures. The polar bear on the top represents the weight of the issue, atop of all the melting. The coral, fish, and sea turtle represent the marine life that is heavily affected. They suggest how species could eventually become lost in space and time. The coffee, butterfly, orchids, and leaf represent the land species affected heavily by this issue. We may have to say goodbye to morning coffee cups, and monarch butterflies if the climate keeps on the current path, but not if we make changes in our lives.

In order to combat this issue, taking small actions such as composting, carpooling, taking your own bags to the grocery store, and growing food from gardens, are stepping stones that can lead to helping our planet. Also, voting for people in office who view climate change as an important topic is a great way to promote a healthier earth. If a large community of people make minor changes in their lifestyle, the outcome could end up being tremendous.

I don't know if teachers really think students like me can write or even think about the world. I am here to say, we do. Don't forget that. I care about the world. I wanted to use my art to show you that.

I was 14 years old when I got interested in sustainability. Before that, I did not understand the full scope of the issue. My brother moved out to Washington. The wind blew up the smoke from the northern region in California up near Seattle, Washington. I learned it was the equivalent of smoking one pack a day. It was the worst trip I have ever gone on. That was the only time there was smoke. We were dropping him off at college for the first time, but I wanted to leave. It is sad to say, but it is true. I started to care about this when it impacted me. I have also gone on a lot of trips about how our region impacts another region. We went to New Mexico and learned about their droughts. They had record-low snowfall and this concerned them with the forest fires. We have Lake Erie and they don't have a water supply. In Costa Rica, we learned about how they produce food. We went to Earth University. They were one of the biggest contributors of growing bananas for Whole Foods. We have machines doing the work, but there, they pick the fruits yourself. The machinery costs money and they spray mass pesticides on everything. That problem is very tricky. In this country, we don't know how to grow these foods to sustain production. In a small country, you can do that and grow food in more sustainable ways, but here, it's more difficult.

This is a social justice issue because in some developing countries, just a minor fluctuation can stop them from producing food at all. In Africa, there are heat waves. The temperature changes are killing people and impacting them. They don't have access to water or clean water and sewage is an issue. If they live by the reefs, they just can't go into the water to fish, because the fish are dying. It's an injustice when we realize that not everyone has basic resources to live life: water, food, shelter.

We should be doing more in schools. In our school, we have a composting system, but in terms of one school, it's not dramatic, but if all schools did this, it would be dramatic. This could mean millions of food and we could make rich soil to make these crops grow. These are the crops that we need. You have to get people to care. That's why I am doing this. If you don't care, then nothing will ever get done. I had to care first too. If I didn't care or don't care about something, I am not going to put effort into it. It's hard. It needs to affect you. I am not sure how to get you to care or to change or to make a difference, but I can show you what's happening. I can show you how it's affecting people. Do you know how bad it is? Here are some things you can do to make a difference in saving our planet.

You can participate in collective action by joining a local grassroots movement or become a volunteer. You can go to marches or stand up for climate change in a protest or speak at a city council meeting or sign petitions or go on social media and educate people. You can have a movie night and show movies like *I am Greta* or *Our Planet* or *Wall-E*. You can talk to politicians and tell them what concerns you and that you want to be involved. You can go online and watch YouTube videos about global awareness. All of us have the power to do something. It's not hard. What will you do?

I liked this art because the artist put words on the forehead (Figure 7.1). It looks like it's crying and there is a poem on the bear. There are smokestacks in the background and I liked that because it demonstrated a cause and an effect. I incorporated the polar bear into my art.

Figure 7.1 Polar bear.

It was kind of the centerpiece because it was at the top of my art. It was mostly because it was on the north pole.

I liked this because it showed how climate change would affect us because she is drowning (Figure 7.2). Maybe that it is going to affect all of us. I liked that it was real water with the art. I didn't use this

Figure 7.2 Lady in water.

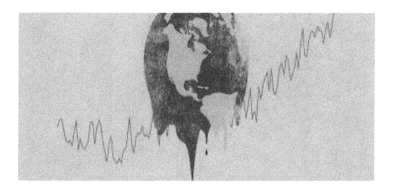

Figure 7.3   The world melts.

symbol in my art. I think I didn't do this because I didn't want this not to be pretty. All of my art in the past was meant to be pretty. I was uncomfortable making art that isn't pretty. This was my first time doing social justice art and social justice isn't pretty. I am not sure how I did it. I think I just pushed through. I had to learn how to be uncomfortable. You can focus on what's good, but you have to know and understand there is bad. When I was uncomfortable, I worked on it alone. I didn't talk about it.

If I were doing this again, I think it's important for students to talk about being uncomfortable. I think we have to be uncomfortable and we are vulnerable and that means we have to talk about things that we don't talk about. At this school and in my family, I am encouraged to talk about things. But in society, boys are taught to be masculine. I think masculine is strong, but not emotions. We are getting better. I would say that most cities have become very liberal.

I liked the graph with the temperature because the graph is going higher, the earth is starting to drip (Figure 7.3). The polar ice caps are melting. I showed the earth melting. I liked that concept (see Figure 7.4).

Conclusion

This art helped me say something about what matters to me—the environment. I am thankful for this chance to show my art. I hope teachers see that students like me think about the world. Don't think that

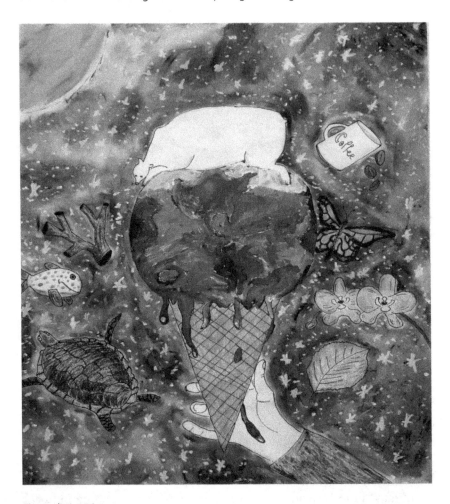

Figure 7.4 The cone.

we don't. I like how it turned out. I hope teachers will give students a chance to do this art. People liked it. I made a difference.

8

Conclusion

Integrating Meaningful Artmaking in Schools

Christa Boske

Integrating the arts throughout schools may not be considered "real work" in some K–12 settings; however, making connections across content while integrating artmaking that reflects real life inspired these young people to engage in learning. Youth came to understand the power of their art in promoting meaningful transformations of self, others, and organizations. This work challenged authors. Justice-oriented artmaking provided them with spaces to promote their ongoing work within and beyond their school community. Artmaking created spaces for youth to communicate their experiences through visual first-tellings, especially when words were not sufficient. Their capacity for artistic expression was evident as they adapted to changing learning conditions and utilized artmaking for problem-solving.

Children With Learning Differences Exploring Artmaking to Address Deficit-Laden Perspectives, pages 67–70
Copyright © 2024 by Information Age Publishing
www.infoagepub.com

For these young authors, artmaking played an integral role in their development of self (see Kaimal, 2019).

The school's capacity to weave artmaking in the very fabric of the educational setting played a critical role in students developing a stronger sense of self and connection with others. Social justice-oriented artmaking provided a myriad of avenues for student learning. Authors discussed the need to promote student-centered work, expressed their capacity to share thoughts and feelings, and explained the extent artmaking encouraged them to contribute to communities and society in meaningful ways.

Authors reiterated how often they were reluctant to share their perspectives with authority figures. Sometimes, youth may resist being told what to do and/or reject redirection or suggestions. This justice-oriented artmaking created spaces for authors to choose topics of interest to them; provided opportunities for teens to make choices and control outcomes; encouraged youth to utilize research-based claims to support their art; and emphasized the need to manipulate materials in meaningful ways. For many of these authors, this arts-based social justice-oriented work invited students to reflect on their lived experiences as students with learning differences and ways in which artmaking created spaces to heal.

It's clear. Integrating artmaking for authors was rarely expected, and oftentimes, engaging in higher-order thinking was not a clear expectation in school (see Anderson, 2015a, 2015b; Loughlin & Anderson, 2015). However, arts integration significantly effects students with learning differences (see Anderson, 2015b; Robinson, 2013). This social justice-oriented artmaking empowered authors and increased their sense of self. They recognized the power they possess to contribute to society in meaningful ways. Authors realize how often they were not afforded opportunities to express themselves, engage in the freedom of artmaking with purpose, and create in nonjudgemental spaces (see Schwartz & Pace, 2008). They stress the need for authentic connections with artmaking. The process seemed to create a bridge between curriculum and collaborative engagement (see Robinson, 2013). This justice-oriented artmaking provided these young people with a bridge between school and self. Youth took ownership of their learning, and of course, for their significant justice-oriented work. Authentically integrating the artmaking through the curriculum provided authors with opportunities to acquire new skills including, but not limited to, research-based art-making, social justice, equity, self-reflection, visual art techniques, and creative writing (Apple, 2006; Schwartz & Pace, 2008).

Educators have a major task: Engage more students in the arts and capture the interests of those they serve by affording them with these opportunities. The process of engaging students in social justice-oriented artmaking emphasizes the significance of high-quality artmaking as well as integrating this meaningful work throughout the curriculum. These authentic connections provided these authors with real-life application, critical thinking, and self-empowerment (see Glass et al., 2013). Authors want to continue to deepen their understanding of the world in which they live; however, teachers and artmaking play a crucial role in this integrated process (see Pennisi, 2012). Teachers choosing to develop these essential skills plays a significant role in supporting this work in schools (Causton-Theoharis & Burdick, 2008).

Promoting democracy in U.S. schools contributes to improving the quality of life for millions of young people. However, financial cutbacks within education may prohibit young people from gaining access to quality arts-based programs. These young authors encourage educators and school leaders to join forces and create an arts-based transformative movement to address the need for meaningful changes in schools. Their artmaking suggests they are ready to act and stress the time is now. Why? The world is changing rapidly. Students recognize artmaking for social justice provides a major opportunity to reassess how schools provide youth with spaces to critically think about identity, self-development, and civic action. Together, they envision new ways to organize these spaces through an integrated curriculum founded in artmaking and the capacity their art holds to greatly influence change in practices, policies, beliefs, and responses, especially for underserved populations.

References

Anderson, A. (2015a). Arts integration as a contextualized language-learning environment. In A. Anderson (Ed.), *Arts integration and special education: An inclusive theory of action for Student Engagement* (pp. 31–45). Routledge.

Anderson, A. (2015b). Understanding how and why arts integration engages learners. In A. Anderson (Ed.), *Arts integration and special education: An inclusive theory of action for Student Engagement* (pp. 59–73). Routledge.

Appel, M. P. (2006). Arts integration across the curriculum. *Leadership, 36*(2), 14–17. https://eric.ed.gov/?id=EJ771707

Causton-Theoharis, J., & Burdick, C. (2008). Paraprofessionals: Gatekeepers of authentic art production. *Studies in Art Education, 49*(3), 167–182. https://www.jstor.org/stable/24467873

Glass, D., Meyer, A., & Rose, D. H. (2013). Universal design for learning and the arts. *Harvard Educational Review, 83*(1), 98–119. https://doi .org/10.17763/haer.83.1.33102p26478p54pw

Kaimal, G. (2019). Adaptive response theory (ART): A clinical research framework for art therapy. *Art Therapy: Journal of the American Art Therapy Association, 36*, 215–219. https://eric.ed.gov/?id=EJ1235278

Loughlin, S. M., & Anderson, A. (2015). A historical review of arts integration research and practice. In A. Anderson (Ed.), *Arts integration and special education: An inclusive theory of action for student engagement* (pp. 5–30). Routledge.

Pennisi, A. C. (2012). A partnership across boundaries: Arts integration in high schools. *Teaching Artist Journal, 10*(2), 102–109. https://doi.org/10 .1080/15411796.2012.658313

Robinson, A. H. (2013). Arts integration and the success of disadvantaged students: A research evaluation. *Arts Education Policy Review, 114*(1), 191–204. https://doi.org/10.1080/10632913.2013.826050

Schwartz, D. C., & Pace, D. (2008). Students create art: Expanding an after-school program. *Teaching Exceptional Children, 40*(4), 50–54. https://doi .org/10.1177/004005990804000406

Printed in the USA
CPSIA information can be obtained
at www.ICGtesting.com
JSHW010352070224
56695JS00003B/19